Walking the K
From End to End

David Bathurst

Photographs by David Bathurst

S. B. Publications

By the same author:

The Selsey Tram
Six Of The Best
The Jennings Companion
Financial Penalties
Around Chichester In Old Photographs
Here's A Pretty Mess!
Magisterial Lore
The Beaten Track
Poetic Justice
That's My Girl
Walking The Coastline Of Sussex
Best Sussex Walks
Let's Take It From The Top
Walking The Disused Railways Of Sussex
Once More From The Top
Sussex Top Tens

To Phil and Julia

First published in 2007 by S.B. Publications
Tel: 01323 893498 Email: sbpublications@tiscali.co.uk

ISBN 978-1-85770-327-6

Typeset by EH Graphics, East Sussex (01273) 515527

CONTENTS

Front Cover: *The twin towers of Reculver.*
Title Page: *The peaceful waters of Stoke Creek.*
Back Cover: *View enjoyed by the walker setting foot for Herne Bay from Reculver.*

ABOUT THE AUTHOR

David Bathurst was born in 1959 and has enjoyed writing and walking throughout his adult life. He has walked all of the principal long-distance footpaths of Great Britain including the Pennine Way, West Highland Way, South West Coast Path, Offa's Dyke Path and the Coast To Coast Walk; he has also walked the entire coastline of Sussex, and his guide to this walk was published by SB Publications in 2002. By profession David is a solicitor and legal adviser to magistrates in Chichester and Worthing. He is married to Susan and has a daughter, Jennifer. When not writing or walking he loves cycling, the works of Gilbert & Sullivan, Flanders and Swann, and the Times crossword puzzle. His most notable achievement was the recital of the four Gospels from memory on a single day in July 1998.

AUTHOR'S ACKNOWLEDGEMENTS

I would like to thank Lindsay Woods of SB Publications for her encouragement and support, and Susan and Jennifer for their love and understanding.

SELECT BIBLIOGRAPHY

Pevsner Architectural Guides - *North East And East Kent/West Kent And The Weald*, John Newman, Yale University Press 2002; *The Companion Guide To Kent And Sussex*, Keith Spence, Companion Guides 1999; *The Saxon Shore Way*, Bea Cowan, Aurum 1996; *Brewer's Britain & Ireland*, John Ayto and Ian Crofton, Weidenfeld & Nicolson 2005.

INTRODUCTION

The coastline of Kent truly has something for everybody. Whether you prefer bracing cliff scenery or a leisurely stroll along a deserted beach or foreshore, bustling seaside resorts with old-fashioned unsophisticated amusements or picturesque chocolate-box towns where time seems to have stood still, historic castles and churches or futuristic late twentieth century feats of engineering, vast swathes of saltmarsh populated with huge numbers of both resident and migrant birds or beautifully-kept seaside gardens and parks, uncompromisingly rough open seas or calm estuarine waters, narrow creeks and inlets full of small sailing boats and leisure craft or large harbours and dockyards capable of accommodating and servicing shipping destined for faraway countries - you will see it all on the 178 miles between the lonely Jury's Gap, within sight of Romney Marsh, and the banks of the river Darent on the outskirts of Dartford.

The Kent coast may lack the drama and unspoilt beauty of coastlines enjoyed by other counties, but it has a fascination that repays considerable and detailed exploration. Standing effectively at the doorway to Great Britain from the Continent, it boasts many fine castles and other ancient defensive fortifications, and has seen the development of several ports of exceptional historical and architectural interest; there are strong associations with many celebrated literary and artistic figures, most notably Charles Dickens who set many of the scenes in his books around the Kent coast; the ravages of the wind and the sea have provided a remarkable variety of coastal landscapes including superb cliffs, marshes, estuaries, creeks and inlets; entrepreneurs who sought to exploit the love of Londoners for bracing sea air have left a rich legacy of architecture; and even more recent phenomena, such as the Channel Tunnel, Dungeness Power Station and the new Queen Elizabeth II bridge, have made their own distinctive mark on the coastline and brought their own type of beauty to the surroundings. The Kent coastline abounds with great sights for the explorer: the castles at Dover, Walmer, Upnor and Rochester, the championship golf course at Sandwich, the twin towers of Reculver, the lovely old towns of Sandwich, Broadstairs and Faversham, the delectable country churches at Cliffe and Harty, the splendid cliff scenery at North Foreland and around Dover, the magnificent Rochester Cathedral, and many, many more.

Arguably the best way to appreciate the Kent coastline is on foot. This book describes a continuous walk from one end of the Kent coast to the other, to be enjoyed not only by budding walkers but also armchair travellers wanting to know more about this very special part of south-east England. There may be some dispute as to where the Kent coast does in fact end, for if by "coast" one thinks in terms of an area of land which faces open sea, it would end in the Sheerness area. For the purpose of this book, however, the term "coast" has been given a broad interpretation, to incorporate the entire estuarine landscape that stretches to the border with the London borough of Bexley at the mouth of the river Darent. The described route is split into 14 sections; the sections are not all of the same length, but there is no reason why the longer sections could not be split into two by walkers who find the distances excessive. I have tried to ensure that each section starts and/or finishes at a place that is well served by public transport, mindful of the fact that many readers will prefer to do the walk in day trips, as indeed I did, rather than tackle the whole walk in one go. Each section begins with a short introduction which advises on distance, route difficulty and public transport for that part of the walk, and there is a separate appendix at the end of the book with a summary of accommodation and refreshment availability.

There is no magic in the choice of route, other than that my aim has been to provide a walk which stays as close to the coastline as possible, without trespassing on to private land. Not all of the described route is along designated rights of way: while there are many coastal paths which aren't shown on maps as rights of way, even though they clearly are, there are some paths, particularly in the latter half of the walk, where access is rather more questionable. Regrettably, one cannot rule out the possibility that changes of land use may result in access to some parts of the described route being debarred, although I have endeavoured to suggest alternative routes where I perceive a real possibility of this. It is most likely to be an issue between Queenborough and Kings Ferry Bridge on the Isle of Sheppey, described in section 10. For the vast majority of the route, there is no difficulty in remaining within sight of the sea on good paths and promenades, with road tramping being kept to an absolute minimum. There will be some seaside stretches where you will be able to follow the beach if you wish, but you must take care not to be cut off by incoming tides.

The walking is not difficult, and indeed in your walking gear you may find yourself somewhat overdressed compared with those you meet strolling along promenades and coastal footpaths in sandals and flipflops. The lack of rough and very hilly terrain, and the generally mild and dry climate, means that heavy walking boots are not required, and indeed I would recommend trainers or stout walking shoes combined with two pairs of socks, a thin inner pair and a thicker outer pair, to guard against blisters. Although in the main you will never be far from shops, pubs and cafes, you are well advised to have supplies of food and drink available, and to start the day with a good breakfast. Try to stick to food that is nutritious as well as high-energy, preferring wholemeal bread and fruit to chocolate and sweets. Make sure you drink plenty of water throughout your walk, especially on hot days, and do not wait till you are thirsty before you do. The text describes the route clearly and succinctly, and you should never get lost, but you may wish to equip yourself with maps, if not for reassurance then for you to follow your progress and identify surrounding landmarks and features of interest. The Ordnance Survey Explorer sheets are the best. Other items to take should include blister treatments (just in case), insect repellent, sun hat and sun cream, sunglasses, camera, binoculars and mobile phone in case of emergency and/or the need for wheeled assistance. Generally public transport links are excellent, but there are some quite remote parts of the coast that are not served by trains or buses, and it may well then be hugely helpful for you to have the means to contact local taxi firms. Please note that in section 13, for the ten miles between Allhallows-on-Sea and Cliffe, the route is completely inaccessible by road, and you should not attempt it unless you are sure you can complete it without recourse to motor transport. However, providing you plan ahead and pace yourself carefully, you will enjoy a great walk round a fascinating coastline.

Happy walking!

David Bathurst, June 2006

One of the many pretty churches close to the Kent coast, the clifftop church at Frindsbury near Strood.

A tranquil spot on the north Kent coast near Faversham.

SECTION 1 - **JURY'S GAP TO DYMCHURCH**

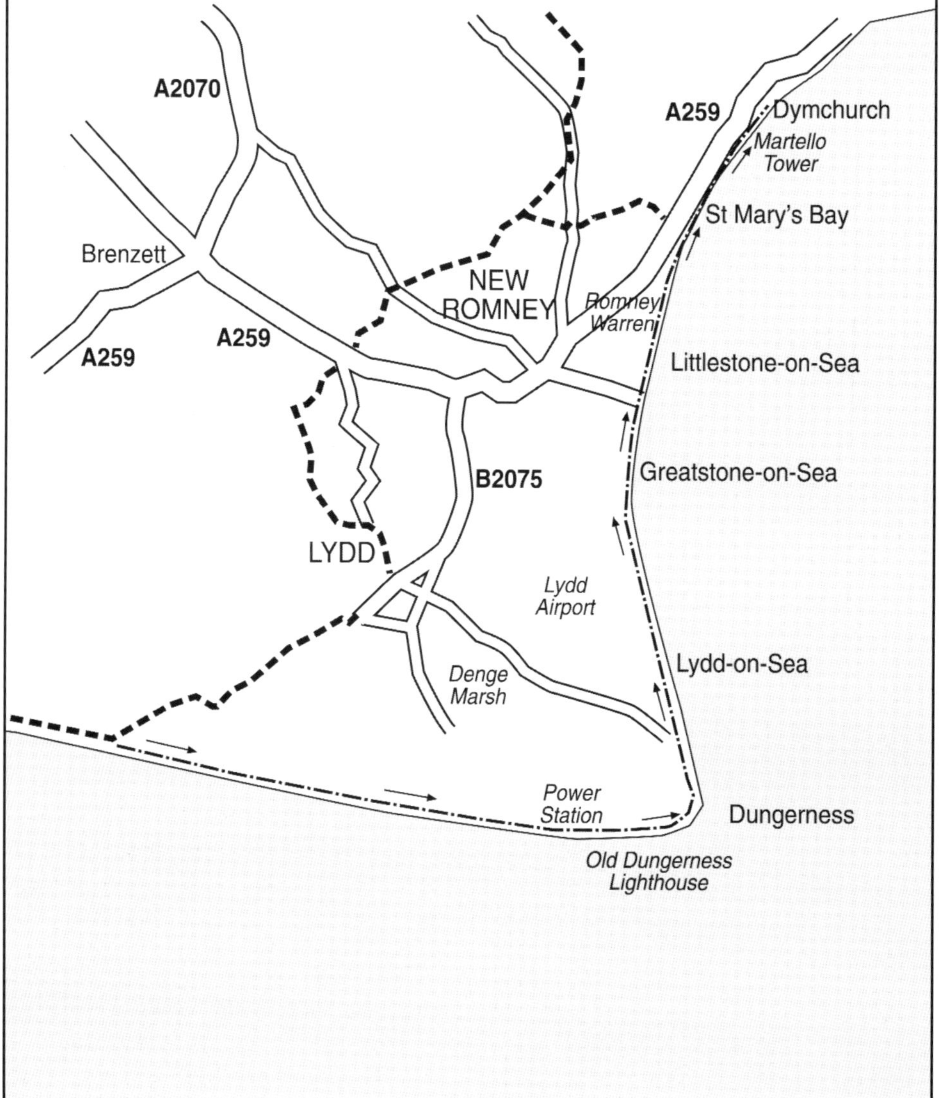

SECTION 1 - **JURY'S GAP TO DYMCHURCH**

Distance:	12 miles
Route:	Jury's Gap - Dungeness - Lydd-on-Sea - Greatstone - Littlestone - St Mary's Bay - Dymchurch.
Maps:	OS Explorer Sheets 125, 138.
Public Transport:	Regular bus services from Hastings and Rye to Dover stopping at Jury's Gap, Lydd, New Romney and Dymchurch. None of the places on or near this section are served by rail, unless you count the Romney, Hythe & Dymchurch Railway which is primarily a tourist attraction and operates in season only; trains on this line run from Dymchurch down to Dungeness.
Conditions:	This is quite a demanding start to your pilgrimage, with a major logistical difficulty right at the start, and some very tough shingle walking towards the middle, but the latter half is easy and straightforward.
Refreshments:	See Appendix.

Your Kent coast pilgrimage must necessarily start in Sussex, since the border between Sussex and Kent is inaccessible by car or public transport. There is a bus stop on the excellent Dover to Hastings service and also car parking at Jury's Gap on the Camber-Lydd road adjoining Broomhill Sands about a mile east of Camber. Shouldering your rucksack or day pack, scramble from the road up on to the shingle, bear left (eastwards) and begin your long walk to Dartford along a coastline that will offer an astonishing variety of landscapes, communities, historical treasures and wildlife.

However, within literally yards of the start, a major logistical problem presents itself. To the left is an Army training area known as the Lydd Ranges, situated on the reclaimed lands of the historic Romney Marsh and part of the cuspate foreland at Dungeness, thought to be between 3000 to 5000 years old. The habitats are of international importance and are part of a special conservation area. The landscape itself has a mystique that is quite eerie; the sense of remoteness is palpable, and it is hard to believe that the seething tourist honeypot of Rye is just four miles away. The area has been used for military training for over 150 years, with one feature of particular interest being the mock-up of an Irish street that has been used for training for Ulster duty. Lydd Ranges are still used for live firing with a Danger Area extending out to sea, and access even along the shingle is prohibited when red flags are flying. It is imperative that you plan your walk along this section for a day when no firing is to take place, as there is no realistic alternative route anywhere near the coast. Weekends and holiday periods offer your best hope, but for further information on live firing times you need to contact 01303 225518 (office hours) or 01303 225467 (out of hours). If it really is totally impossible to coincide your walk along this section with a time when the ranges are open, you will need to follow the road from Jury's Gap north-eastwards all the way to Lydd, then follow the road down to Lydd-on-Sea to pick up the coast path. It is a long road trudge, the only compensation being in the form of Lydd itself, which boasts an 18th century town hall and a magnificent church that is of Saxon origin, 199ft long and with a west tower 132ft high.

Assuming all is well, proceed along the metalled track towards the MOD installation which marks the start of the restricted area. Beyond it, you have the choice of staying on the track or dropping down to the shore. It is suggested that you begin along the track, from which you get a good view of the Lydd Ranges and the countryside beyond it, as well as the sea; you will also be able to look out across the vast expanse of Romney Marsh. Pause here before proceeding further, as Romney Marsh is a fascinating area in its own right albeit not part of your coastal walk as such. The area was originally a saltmarsh but was reclaimed from the sea long ago and is now a mixture of arable land and grazing pasture, home to one of the world's best known breeds of sheep, the white-faced Romney Marsh sheep. The area is exceedingly rich in bird life, which may include wintering lapwings, golden plovers, Bewick's swans, lapwings, migrant fieldfares and redwings, swallows, wagtails and nightingales. One creature of particular interest is the marsh frog, initially introduced to this area in 1935. Enjoy the view of Romney Marsh while you can; before long the shingle bank to your right becomes too tall to view the sea properly, so use one of the paths across the shingle depression to your right to access the bank and then make your way to the shore. Imperceptibly, you pass from Sussex into Kent, and your Kent coast walk is truly under way. The sand/shingle mix is reasonably firm so you can make progress without difficulty; only if the tide is right up may you be forced on to the bank and progress will then be extremely slow. The sense of remoteness and timelessness is quite palpable, with precious few landmarks or people, or indeed any reminders of the trappings of twenty-first century life. It is an almost surreal start to a walk which will in due course see you passing through some of the most bustling coastal settlements in the southern half of England.

Eventually, some five miles of shore walking from Jury's Gap, you draw level with the Dungeness nuclear power stations. If you are walking along the shore you will only be able to see the topmost funnel from the shoreline.

Dungeness

Dungeness is a remarkable place and although your walk has barely started, you may wish to stop here for closer exploration. A lighthouse was first built here in 1615, at a time when it is said that 1000 persons perished here for want of light each year. Latterly, there have been two lighthouses and the base of a third, made into a circular house. The modern lighthouse, opened in 1960, is a most impressive construction, worked from complex control panels in its base and boasting a new slim floodlit tower banded black and white, built up of prestressed concrete rings. Pevsner describes it as "excellent(and) immaculately shipshape, shaming the scruffy shacks that surround them and sprawl for miles northwards up the coast."

Dungeness is dominated by its two power stations, Dungeness A and Dungeness B. Power Station A was built in the early 1960's and Pevsner describes it as "aesthetically a disappointment,"commenting on its positively Palladian symmetry and the "disturbing clutter of wires and pylons all around...striding insensitively across Romney Marsh."Power Station B was built in the late 1960's and was planned to be the most powerful nuclear power station in the world. It may be possible to join a guided tour or visit the large information centre. Besides the power stations, there is an important 12,000-acre bird reserve nearby at Denge Marsh, from which Dungeness gets its name, and Dungeness is the southern terminus of the Romney, Hythe & Dymchurch Railway, about which more below. Fishing from the shore is excellent, although bathing and boating are rendered hazardous by the strong currents. In World War 2 Dungeness housed one of the two northern terminals for PLUTO, an acronym for Pipe Line Under The Ocean, which was an underwater oil supply pipe carrying petrol from England to northern France in the wake of the D-day landings.

The whole area is of great interest for birdwatchers. Black redstarts actually breed among the buildings of the power station, and kestrels perch on the pylons. The shores around Dungeness provide a significant migration watchpoint, with many rare birds to be seen including Pallas' warblers and red-breasted flycatchers, and butterfly enthusiasts will be drawn in the summer to the hordes of painted lady or clouded yellow butterflies. The flooded gravel pits, testimony to years of commercial gravel extraction, provide the most important bird habitat hereabouts, with a rich variety of wildfowl and waders all through the year. As well as smew, terns and grebes, there are crowds of gulls to be seen including dark-hooded Mediterranean gulls, which are to be found on only comparatively few other sites in Britain.

The great shingle spit here, deposited by the sea over a period of 400 years, is four miles deep, and increasing all the time; its flora is surprisingly varied with over 400 recorded species, notably the carpets of thrift, stonecrop, sea kale and sea campion.

When you draw level with the power station, clamber up on to the shingle bank. Suddenly the vista changes completely and on a clear day you will get a marvellous panoramic view of the Kent coast as far as Shakespeare Cliff between Folkestone and Dover as well as the untidy assortment of houses and boats in the immediate vicinity of Dungeness. Now you literally turn the corner, so your direction of travel goes from just south of east to north. Your reward is an extremely tough section of shingle walking from which there is no easy escape; this is one of the hardest sections of the entire walk. Look out, however, for the garden on the shingle created by the late Derek Jarman, a film-maker who moved here in 1986. Plod on, taking care not to trip on the many ropes and wires surrounding the boats planted on the shingle; there are some firmer sections among the mass of stones but you have to look hard for them! Aim for the very conspicuous RNLI station, the tarmac forecourt providing a brief respite from the shingle tramping, but having passed the station to the seaward side you then face more walking over shingle. Finally you arrive at the Pilot public house - you may feel you've deserved a drink here after all your hard work - and meet the road coming in from the left which swings north-eastwards at the Pilot to become a coast road. This is Lydd-on-Sea, a very straggly village indeed with no features of interest, although there is the possibility of a bus from here to the town of Lydd, referred to above, with its superb church.

At Lydd-on-Sea you have a choice. You could follow the coast road or the shingle bank that is across the shingle to the right of the road (note that some areas of this shingle are privately owned). This is extremely tough going, but there is the possibility of being able to access the sands providing the tide is not too high. Now simply follow the road, bank (giving way to dunes) or sands past the equally straggly community of Greatstone-on-Sea. Architecturally there is nothing of any interest here at all, Pevsner dismissing it as a collection of beach houses and bungalows "developed between the wars in the Peacehaven mood" which was certainly not intended as a compliment, but at low tide you may observe a sunken section of the World War 2 Mulberry Harbour which did not make it to the Normandy beaches. During the days of smuggling the sand dunes here offered good cover for those occupied in the trade. Continue forward to Littlestone-on-Sea, a greensward just beyond the lifeboat station providing relief from the shingle. Described by Keith Spence as possessing "an air of faded Victorian gentility," with its pink granite Diamond Jubilee fountain in front of the hotels, the village has little more to recommend it architecturally than Greatstone. It became a popular residential resort in the 1890's and boasted a seafront Grand Hotel, which was opened in 1891, as well as a 45-bed convalescent home for women and girls which was opened in 1902 with the object of giving patients the benefit of healthy sea breezes! Pevsner is little more complimentary about it than about Greatstone, alluding to its rows of boarding houses three, four or five storeys high, "bleakly facing the sea." It is possible to detour here on to the B2071 which in just over a mile brings you to New Romney.

Romney and the Cinque Ports

Romney was one of the original Cinque(pronounced "sink" from the French word for "five") Ports, to which there will be a number of references as you read on. The Cinque Ports was the original collective name, from the 11th century, for the five Kent and Sussex seaports of Sandwich, Dover, Hythe and Hastings as well as Romney, which were granted special privileges through their provision of men and ships for the defence of the Channel. Subsequently Rye and Winchelsea were added and ultimately there were 32 lesser members of the incorporated body including Deal, Folkestone, Margate and Faversham. Their

The Assembly Rooms in Church Approach, Romney, with the Norman church of St Nicholas in the background.

privileges were largely surrendered in 1685 and some are not even by the sea any more, as a result of silting. However there is still such an office as Lord Warden of the Cinque Ports. Romney is perhaps the least distinguished of the original Cinque Ports, and is one of those that is not even by the sea at all: its harbour was destroyed by a storm in 1287 which diverted the course of the River Rother to Rye, and with the sea receding, the town is now some way inland. The present New Romney in fact consists of the amalgamation of the town of Romney with Littlestone-on-Sea and Greatstone-on-Sea. The little town of Romney (confusingly marked on maps as New Romney, while the village of Old Romney lies well over a mile further inland to the west) is certainly worth a detour. Its principal attraction is the magnificent Norman church of St Nicholas, originally built between 1160 and 1170 and enlarged eastwards in the 14th century; it has got a particularly fine tower and west door. At the time of the Domesday Book there were 3 parish churches, a priory and a hospital in the town, but St Nicholas was the only church still extant by the late 16th century. Other buildings of interest in the town include the Assembly Rooms, with its fine early 18th century brick front, and the yellow-brick 1676 School Room, both in Church Approach; a timber-framed hall house in the High Street with the curious name Electric House; the late 19th century Town Hall and the red-brick seven-bayed Priory House, both also in the High Street; the medieval St John's Priory in Ashford Road; and two sets of 18th century almshouses, one in West Street and one in St John's Road. In addition, the town offers a good range of amenities, provides excellent bus links to Rye and Folkestone, and has a station on the Romney, Hythe & Dymchurch Railway (see Dymchurch below).

Beyond the greensward at Littlestone the going gets extremely easy, as there is now a proper concrete coast path running all the way to St Mary's Bay. You pass a very conspicuous late 19th century tower, which you will love or hate, and the excellent Littlestone golf course, the first of many highly rated golf courses you will meet on your Kent coastal walk. The golf club dates back to 1888, and one club handbook of

The splendid tower of the Norman church of St Nicholas, Romney, the only survivor of 3 parish churches that existed at the time of the Domesday Book.

yesteryear invited golfers to pause awhile on the 17th tee and, among other things, "discern, if you can, the coast of France on a clear day." Though the chances of your being able to look right across the Channel are slim, the views across to Hythe, Folkestone, the North Downs and Shakespeare Cliff just west of Dover are superb. Continue along the coast path, passing the houses of St Mary's Bay, and now walking along an impressively wide promenade which gives you wonderfully easy marching, in marked contrast to the shingle walking a few miles back. St Mary's Bay was once the home of Noel Coward, who lived in a converted stable, and the children's author Edith Nesbit, who wrote *The Railway Children*. She lived with her husband Captain Tucker at The Long Boat until her death in 1924. From St Mary's Bay the walking remains very easy all the way on to Dymchurch. On arrival at Dymchurch, it is a very short walk down the slip road to its centre and the many amenities it offers, including several cafes.

Dymchurch

Dymchurch was once a smuggling port, and its connection with smugglers was the basis of the stories by Russell Thorndike of the mythical Dr Syn, a smuggling parson. It was more prosaically the meeting place of the Lords of the Level who looked after the drainage of the Romney Marshes; it lies seven feet below the high water mark but enjoys the protection of a huge sea-barrier known as Dymchurch Wall which was first constructed by the Romans. Dymchurch is now predominantly a little seaside resort with safe bathing and good shore fishing including shrimping available. Arguably the most interesting aspect of Dymchurch as a coastal settlement is its Martello Tower, an English Heritage site with many exhibits showing preparations to deal with prospective Napoleonic invaders. It is one of three Martello Towers in the vicinity of the village; the Martello Towers were a line of about 70 circular defence towers that were built along the Sussex and Kent coast between 1805 and 1808 as a defence against the threat of French invasion. They were round towers of solid masonry, sometimes moated, with a flat roof for guns. Other highlights of Dymchurch are its church which although altered significantly in 1821 contains some Norman work, including a fine Norman south doorway; the Ship Inn which was famous for its association with smugglers (the Lords, Bailiff

Full steam ahead on the Romney, Hythe & Dymchurch: a train leaves Dymchurch for Hythe on a hot July afternoon.

and Jurats of Romney Marsh used to hold their annual lunch there, turning a blind eye to smuggling activities!); the 18th century New Hall opposite the church with its old Court Room of the Lords of the Level containing simple 18th century seating and the royal arms of George II of 1739; and a stop on the Romney, Hythe & Dymchurch Railway. One of the best known and best loved steam railways in the country, it was built as a tourist attraction in 1929; its engines are replicas of London North Eastern expresses and other locomotives at one third full size, it has a gauge of just fifteen inches, and it runs for 13 miles, starting at Hythe and terminating at Dungeness. The station stop at Dymchurch is particularly conveniently sited for coastal walkers who fancy letting the train take the strain! The line was considered so strategically important in World War 2 that it was requisitioned by the Army, with material being transported along the railway to the Dungeness terminal of PLUTO (see above). Dymchurch is an extremely popular holiday village, boasting a great many holiday homes and in the summer and on Bank Holidays the streets likely to be packed with visitors; there is, it has to be said, a rather tacky feel to the shops and cafes adjoining the slip road down to the main street. It is, however, a convenient place to end this section, with excellent bus links to Folkestone, Romney, Rye and Hastings.

Reposing in the engine shed at Romney station, this is one of the splendid fleet of miniature locomotives on the Romney, Hythe & Dymchurch Railway, each a one third size replica of a full-sized steam locomotive.

SECTION 2 - **DYMCHURCH TO DOVER**

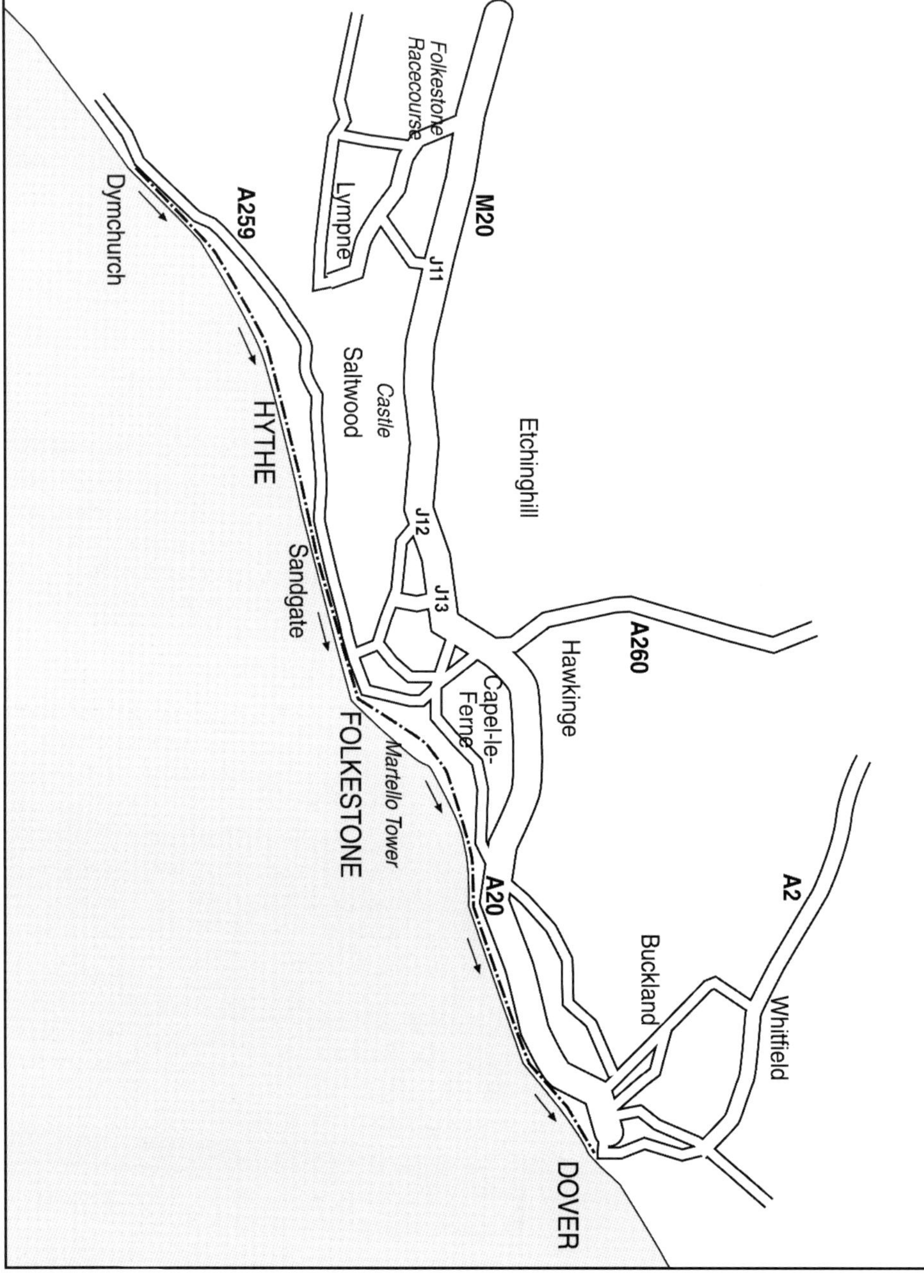

SECTION 2 - **DYMCHURCH TO DOVER**

Distance:	16 miles.
Route:	Dymchurch - Hythe - Sandgate - Folkestone East Cliff - Battle Of Britain Memorial - Shakespeare Cliff - Dover.
Map:	OS Explorer Sheet 138.
Public Transport:	Excellent bus service between Dover and Hastings which serves both Dymchurch and Folkestone. Regular trains from Folkestone to Dover, Ashford and London Charing Cross. Regular trains (half-hourly Mon-Sat) from Dover to London Victoria via Canterbury and Faversham.
Conditions:	The first half consists of very easy level walking throughout, on firm surfaces, albeit with one major logistical difficulty (see text). The second half contains some magnificent cliff walking and the section ends with the most interesting single location on the whole walk. It is perfectly feasible to break the section in two with a stopover at Folkestone.
Refreshments:	See Appendix.

Leaving Dymchurch, you simply continue along a good concrete path by the back of the beach, making excellent progress; the suburban housing immediately to the left presents as a stark contrast to the barren landscape that characterised the early part of the previous section. Continue along Dymchurch Wall, and in just under 2 miles you reach the Dymchurch Redoubt and the entrance to the Hythe Ranges. An area of low lying, slightly undulating land adjoining the foreshore, Hythe Ranges comprise one of the oldest firing ranges in the country, having been used for live firing for nearly 200 years. On the Ranges there are three Scheduled Ancient Monuments. Unfortunately, the Ranges present you with another logistical difficulty, in that they are still used for live firing today, with a Danger Area extending out to sea; firing takes place on most days and when it does, the area is then out of bounds. To enquire about live firing times, contact 01303 225879 (office hours) or 01303 225861 (out of hours). If you have planned your visit carefully and the ranges are open, proceed round the beach side of the MOD buildings, walking across slippery stones to join a track that continues for two miles along the back of the beach with good views to the ranges and street mock-ups. Beyond the ranges a Martello Tower blocks the way straight ahead; go down

The splendid view of Folkestone from the Leas, an expanse of lawns and flower gardens on the clifftops, and hugely popular with locals and visitors. Nearby to where this picture is taken is Leas Cliff Hall, a fine conference and concert venue.

on to the beach and almost at once scramble back on to a concrete path* taking you forward to Hythe. The path bypasses the centre of Hythe and if you wish to stop to visit the town you will need to bear left up St Leonards Road which takes you into the centre. (NOTE: If you have not been so fortunate and firing is taking place, you will need to make your way from the Redoubt to the adjacent A259 and follow it all the way past Pennypot into Hythe itself, forking right off Dymchurch Road into Portland Road and then first right into St Leonards Road which takes you down to the concrete path asterisked above. The detour, although giving you the chance to visit Hythe, will add a good extra mile to your journey. The moral is to avoid firing days!)

Hythe

Although it is now somewhat set back from the sea through silting and the build-up of shingle, Hythe was the central port of the five original Cinque Ports. The harbour it once boasted has now long gone, but the strategic associations remain, for Hythe stands at the eastern end of the Royal Military Canal, built in 1807 as a response to the threat of invasion during the Napoleonic Wars. William Cobbett, author of Rural Rides, *was extremely disparaging about the effectiveness of the canal, 30ft wide at most, to deter potential invaders who would have negotiated the Rhine or the Danube en route to England! The canal is now something of a tourist attraction, lined as it is with trees and flowers; it has been popular with fishermen and a water pageant has been a regular feature here in recent years.*

The town contains many delightful features besides the tree-shaded canal. There is a long narrow High Street with narrow alleys leading off it, and a pretty grid of streets and lanes between the High Street and the church of St Leonard; the church itself, which dates back to the 12th century, is described by Pevsner as once having had the grandest chancel of any non-monastic church in the county. The chancel was built in about 1220 but it was not finally vaulted until 1886, and the church tower was destroyed by an earth tremor in 1739 and rebuilt in 1750. The church crypt, reached from outside the church, contains a macabre mystery in the form of 2000 human skulls and 8000 thigh bones which scientists say are of a different type from any other found almost anywhere in Britain. Buried in the churchyard is Lionel Lukin, who invented the lifeboat, and appropriately enough Hythe had its own lifeboat although the lifeboat house was built some way to the east of the town. Other buildings of interest include the 18th century Old Manor House, the early 19th century Hill House, the Town Hall which dates back to 1794, and the fine Westminster Bank building of 1912. The town marks the eastern terminus of the Romney, Hythe & Dymchurch Railway (see above). There is a considerable amount of modern housing, which, like the town centre, is set well back from the sea: Pevsner amusingly writes that Hythe now has "houses for those who want to see the sea in their retirement, but keep a distance from it." Indeed a number of private hotels were developed in the town and it became popular with retired colonial servants and military officers.

If you have time, you may wish to detour a mile inland to Saltwood, where you will find the ruins of an early Norman castle which was damaged by an earthquake in the late 16th century. The four knights who murdered Thomas a Becket stayed at the castle on the night before the murder.

Continue along the concrete path, passing the Hotel Imperial and a golf course, and now heading for the Sandgate and Folkestone conurbation. About two miles beyond Hythe the A259 comes in from the left and as you reach a garage you find yourself walking along the roadside pavement into Sandgate at the western end of Folkestone, still with the beach to your right. However in a little over half a mile the A259 becomes separated from the beach by buildings, and you now leave the A259 to follow another concrete path along the back of the beach. Soon you pass Sandgate Castle lying to your left.

Sandgate

Sandgate Castle was one of a series of castles built by Henry VIII between 1539 and 1540; in 1806 the central core was converted into a gunfort, and it became effectively a Martello Tower (see above). In 1820 a landing was carried out close to Sandgate Castle involving 300 smugglers, leading to a pitched battle with excise officials. During the last war, the nearby beach was covered in obstacles including barbed wire to prevent invasion. Sandgate itself, apart from a number of weatherboarded cottages in its High Street (off route), has little else of architectural or historic interest, although nearby are the big Shorncliffe barracks that were also built as part of Napoleonic defences, and from which troops were sent to France during the First World War, many fated never to return. Spade House, in Radnor Cliff Crescent, was the seaside hide-out of the novelist H.G. Wells whose book Kipps, which inspired the musical Half A Sixpence, was set in and around Folkestone; the Radnor Cliff area itself has been home to many of the Folkestone area's wealthier residents. The fishing at Sandgate has been very good, with regular catches of plaice, conger and codling, and the invigorating sea air prompted the building of the Beach House Convalescent Home here in 1890, supported by the London Samaritan Society.

The cliff railway which provides access to the Leas from the seaside promenades at Folkestone is one of the town's most distinctive visitor attractions.

Continue along the concrete path, now heading for Folkestone. A little further on to your right are the rocks of Mill Point and the paraphernalia of an elaborate flood defence scheme, and as your path bends slightly to the left, you can now see more of the buildings of central Folkestone. Note also the cliff railway to your left, linking the seaside promenade with the Leas (see below). Shortly the concrete path gives way to a large open area where markets are regularly held and a little beyond that are some rather antiquated fairground attractions. You are now approaching a dead end so you need to turn left and pass between the amusements to join the harbourside road. Turn right on to it; very soon it swings sharply left, marked on the map here as the Harbour Approach Road, and suddenly you find yourself facing the town's harbour and surrounding buildings. Walk beside the water and soon reach a cobbled area on your right which is enormously popular at holiday times, with stalls selling seafood. The shopping centre of Folkestone can be reached by crossing over via Harbour Street and going forward into Tontine Street.

Folkestone

The name of Folkestone in Saxon times was Fulchestane, believed to mean " a piece of rock where folk met together." Although it was granted a licence for its own port in 1629, and became one of the Cinque Ports, Folkestone's real prosperity began with the arrival of the railway and the growth of the cross-Channel passenger service in the 19th century; previously it had consisted of little more than an accumulation of fishermen's cottages by the harbour and a few houses round the church. The town has in fact always maintained a strong fishing community.

The railway transformed Folkestone and it became an extremely popular seaside resort, with good beaches, all the traditional seaside attractions and, along the top of the cliffs, a very special area known as the Leas, consisting of an expanse of lawns and flower gardens separated from the sea-level promenades by a tangle of broom and pine trees. The town has a number of famous associations: it was the birthplace of the actress Audrey Hepburn, the short-story writer Alfred Edgar Coppard, and the sometime New Zealand prime minister Sir William Hall-Jones, it was the home of the novelist H.G. Wells (see above), and Charles Dickens rented a property here when writing his novel Little Dorrit. Folkestone's most famous son was the biologist William Harvey who discovered the circulation of the blood, and who was born here in 1578. He died in London in 1657, possibly by taking poison after he found he was going blind. In the Leas there is a statue of William Harvey, holding a heart in his hand.

Architecturally there are no really outstanding buildings in Folkestone - as stated above, it was only in the Victorian age that Folkestone expanded significantly as a town - although the church on the hilltop stands amid attractive weatherboarded and Georgian redbrick buildings, and there is a certain charm about the narrow steep High Street even though many of the cottages have been gutted to create souvenir shops or restaurants. The church, an Early English (i.e. immediately post-Norman) building has an unusual dedication, to St Mary and St Eanswythe, the latter being the first English princely abbess. A lead casket, thought to contain her relics, was found in 1885 in the north wall of the chancel, and remains there today. There is also a window in the church in memory of William Harvey (see above). There are considerable numbers of prominent Victorian buildings in the town, and standing out amongst the 20th century edifices is Leas Cliff Hall, an important concert and conference venue that was opened in 1927. The Leas itself could be said to be the town's biggest "draw,"

The harbour at Folkestone, dotted with boats and dominated by the railway which brought prosperity to the town in the 19th century.

and Keith Spence sums its charms up thus: "For any South Coast resort to compare itself to the Bay of Naples may seem far-fetched; yet if you look over the treetops on a sunny afternoon to some lonely fisherman in a dinghy far below, the scene is much more Mediterranean than the English Channel."

The most significant development in Folkestone's recent history has been the opening of the Eurotunnel terminal and exhibition centre illustrating the building of the Channel tunnel. The terminal is in fact situated at Cheriton, just to the north of the town. The tunnel itself was opened by Queen Elizabeth II on 6th May 1994.

To continue your coastal walk from the harbour at Folkestone, turn right through the cobbled area off Harbour Street to join the Fish Market, itself a cobbled street which passes under the redbrick railway arches and beside further fish sellers and attractive redbrick houses. Go past a sign pointing to East Cliff and The Warren; the cobbled street becomes a concrete path which keeps close to the beach, and as you follow this path you will enjoy fine views to the cliffs ahead. Shortly beyond a café and toilets turn left as signposted up a flight of steps to reach an area of green on the cliffs, then turn right to walk along the green, passing to the cliff side of a building prominently marked THE PAVILION. You soon join a metalled track and shortly arrive at a signpost pointing you left to the Martello Tower Visitor Centre and Warren Birdlife Trail. (The Visitor Centre, built inside a Martello Tower, provides a history of these fortifications.) Bear left as signed, and return to the cliff edge, then keeping the cliff edge immediately to your right, continue forward across the green area, going downhill and to the right of some enclosed greens. Shortly beyond is the site of a Roman villa which was occupied between 100-350 AD. You ascend, continuing in the same direction, but then as you get towards the top end of the green you need to walk diagonally left, passing below and in front of another Martello Tower, to arrive at a narrow metalled road. Turn right on to the road and follow it uphill, then, as it bends right, join a narrow path which carries on in the same direction you have been taking. Follow this path steeply uphill.

This is the most adventurous and spectacular walking so far. Below you is the Folkestone-Dover railway, and to your right is the Warren, a landslip basin and extraordinary wilderness area between the cliffs and the sea, rich in plant and bird life; there are rare plants, hundreds of trees and shrubs, and fossils. Formed by a series of landfalls over the past 4000 years, caused by chalk movement and shingle drift, it is a particularly popular area with bird lovers, who come to watch the hordes of migrating birds and to hear the nightingale and chiffchaff. Continue uphill to reach a T-junction at which you turn right; you have now reached the North Downs Way which you will follow all the way to the outskirts of Dover. The North Downs Way, running to Dover from Farnham, Surrey, was opened in 1978 and provides a challenging walk across the Surrey Hills and the Kent Downs. You also here join the Saxon Shore Way, a 163-mile route linking Gravesend and Hastings, with which the Kent coast will overlap considerably over the ensuing miles. Go forward along the path to arrive on the clifftop, then bear left (north-eastwards) to head towards Dover.

The going is now very easy as you simply follow the North Downs Way as directed by the waymarks for that path. Almost immediately you notice the very impressive Battle Of Britain Memorial to your left; completed in 1993, it comprises a large aircraft propeller with blades forty yards long cut into the grass, and on the central boss there is a sculpture depicting a Battle of Britain fighter pilot. The Memorial continues to be used today as a navigational aid. Then simply keep to the clifftop path, avoiding paths leading down into the Warren, unless of course you wish to make the detour. The only slight deviation from the clifftop comes when about a mile and a half beyond the memorial you are forced a little inland to bypass some buildings, but even then you are soon reunited with the clifftop and continue resolutely on. This is tremendous walking - some might argue that there is nothing better to come, although that is a matter of opinion! - with glorious sea views and the Warren immediately below you. Those who suffer from vertigo might indeed want to keep back a little, as the drop from just a few yards to the right can seem very stark. And those who think that romance has gone from rail travel might think again as they observe the trains on the Folkestone-Dover route plying an intricate and extraordinarily beautiful route through the Warren far below; in fact railway ventilation shafts appear along the clifftops from time to time. As you continue, look out on the right for Samphire Hoe, a broad chalk platform formed from the vast tonnage of chalk - 4 million cubic metres in all! - dug from the Channel Tunnel workings. It stands on the foreshore behind a new sea wall and has been landscaped, with rye grass and other local plants being encouraged to grow around the site. The large grassy areas, interspersed with gravel paths, have made it a popular country park and picnic spot, and far below you can see the car park and visitors enjoying this new leisure

The lighthouse at Samphire Hoe, a broad chalk platform created by the chalk dug from the Channel Tunnel workings, and now a landscaped country park and major visitor attraction.

facility. It is named after the samphire gatherer spotted by Edgar in King Lear, part of the action of which takes place on the cliffs a little further east (see below). The picturesque church you can see over the fields to your left is the Norman church of St Lawrence the Martyr at Church Hougham, once used by smugglers for concealing contraband.

Looking to your left, you will see the main A20, which has been close at hand for much of your cliff walk, beginning to descend towards Dover, and you will also see some of the buildings of Dover ahead of you. Before plunging down into this immensely important and interesting town, you must negotiate the last and best-known cliff on this section, namely Shakespeare Cliff. This sheer cliff is one of the legendary White Cliffs of Dover, immortalised in song by Vera Lynn; for centuries these cliffs have symbolised both Britain's defiance of potential invaders and the promise of homecoming for weary voyagers. The cliff was the setting, in Shakespeare's King Lear, for the scene in which Edgar urges the blind Gloucester to plunge to his death. Until the mid-1990's, Shakespeare Cliff marked the official end of the North Downs Way but the trail has since been extended into Dover, via a somewhat disappointing suburban route. Having made your way over this final clifftop, descend, now enjoying sumptuous views to Dover and its surroundings. As you reach the bottom of the cliff, still quite a way above the sea, you will notice the North Downs Way signposted as going off left beneath an underpass below the A20; do not take this route, but instead continue parallel with the A20 and very soon you reach a flight of steps going off to your right downhill. Take these steps which lead you over the railway and down to the beach, then turn left to follow the beach towards Dover. This will be your first piece of beach walking since Littlestone, and if the tide is in you will find yourself with a tough tramp over the shingle. Soon, however, a concrete path is available, and the going becomes easier; follow the path until you can go no further, with the way ahead effectively blocked by the Western Docks. Turn left and go forward to shortly reach a roundabout, at which you take the signed A20 Folkestone exit; although this is an important thoroughfare for motor traffic entering and leaving the Western Docks you will be relieved to hear that there is a pavement. Soon you reach another roundabout, the Limekiln Roundabout, at which you turn right to follow beside the A20, the main waterfront road, using the pavement on the harbour side. Very soon you reach a third roundabout, marked on maps as the Prince Of Wales Roundabout, and here you turn right into Union Street, using the cycle path. In a few yards you arrive at the waterfront proper, and you turn left to follow the Esplanade, with the Outer Harbour to your right. This is lovely relaxing walking after the slogging past all the roundabouts. Although your coastal walk continues along the front, by way of the Esplanade, Waterloo Crescent and Marine Parade, you will surely want to use one of the roads or walkways leading off to the left hereabouts to detour to Dover's many amenities and fascinating buildings.

Dover

Dover is undoubtedly the most interesting town you will meet on your coastal walk. Though not a huge town - its population can be measured in tens rather than hundreds of thousands - it is the world's busiest passenger port and England's principal cross-Channel port. At the start of the 21st century 16 million passengers and 2 million vehicles were passing through the port every year. The vast expanse of Dover harbour is in fact comparatively new, the present layout dating only from the early 20th century and designed to accommodate the whole British fleet. Dover is also a busy workaday town, with industries which include electronics, paper manufacturing and light engineering.

The strategic importance of Dover - with France just 21 miles away across the Channel, it is Britain's nearest point to mainland Europe - has been recognised for thousands of years. The town, one of the original Cinque Ports, has been described by Matthew Paris as the "front door of England" and thus the obvious entry point to Britain for would-be invaders. In the last war it was known as "Hellfire Corner" because of the number of attacks on the town. There was a pre-Roman settlement here; when the Romans arrived they called the town Portus Dubris, and in about 50 AD they established a beacon or "lighthouse" in what was to become the grounds of the Norman castle. The 62 ft high lighthouse, or Pharos as it is known, is one of the oldest Roman buildings in the country and it is remarkable that it can still be seen today. The lower part of the lighthouse has been magnificently preserved. The other outstanding Roman building still to be seen in Dover is the Roman Painted House, built in around 200 AD; an exhibition in the house describes the Roman occupation and includes Roman wall paintings. The impressive museum in Market Square offers a wide range of exhibits that bring Dover's past to life, including a Bronze Age boat, while the White Cliffs Experience provides a more interactive introduction to Dover's history and surroundings.

The main attraction of Dover is its Norman castle, built on cliffs overlooking the town on the site of earlier fortifications and remaining a vitally important defensive garrison for centuries. It is renowned for its magnificent and richly-decorated keep, built by Henry II in 1180's; the walls of the keep are between 17 and 22 ft thick. Spence describes it as a "classic of castle building (of) immense strength" and offering "magnificent living accommodation." The castle was later requisitioned by Oliver Cromwell in the English Civil War and was subsequently strengthened to counter the threat from Napoleonic forces. During World War 2, the elaborate network of tunnels under the castle, built during the time of the Napoleonic wars, was used as the control base for the Dunkirk evacuation. From the castle keep there are extensive views which on a clear day can extend to the French coast. Also within the castle grounds is the really fine Saxon church of St Mary in Castro. Pevsner describes the church as being THE outstanding late Saxon building in the county. One other very significant piece of evidence of Dover's defensive past is the assembly of Napoleonic War fortifications on the Western Heights, the brick casements and redoubts standing out impressively above the surrounding buildings.

There are a number of other buildings of note in the town. The parish church of St Mary, in Cannon Street, has a Norman tower and Norman arches, and it also has a window commemorating the victims of the Zeebrugge ferry disaster in 1987. Nearby is the Victorian Town Hall in Biggin Street which incorporates the medieval Maison Dieu hospital and the old town gaol. The hospital was founded around 1221 not only for the poor and infirm but also pilgrims of whom there were many passing through Dover on their way to the Continent from Canterbury, and vice versa. The 13th century St Edmund's Chapel in Priory Road, was consecrated in 1253 and is believed to be the smallest church in regular use in the country; opposite is Maison Dieu House, now the Public Library, which dates back to 1665 and which boasts an excellent brick-built façade; and the chiefly 19th century Dover College in Effingham Crescent incorporates the remains of St Martin's Priory, which was founded as long ago as 1131. The refectory survives in toto, and it is described by Pevsner as being one of the most impressive mid-12th century domestic buildings in the country.

Dover's position so close to France makes it a natural departure point for Channel swimmers, and indeed Matthew Webb began the first ever recorded Channel swim from Dover in 1875. Louis Bleriot's cross-Channel flight, the first such flight in history, ended near Dover on 25th July 1909, and a granite shape in North Fall Meadow marks the site where he landed.

The fine view out to sea from the popular Leas Promenade at Folkestone.

Fishing is one of the many leisure pursuits enjoyed at Samphire Hoe.

SECTION 3 - **DOVER TO DEAL**

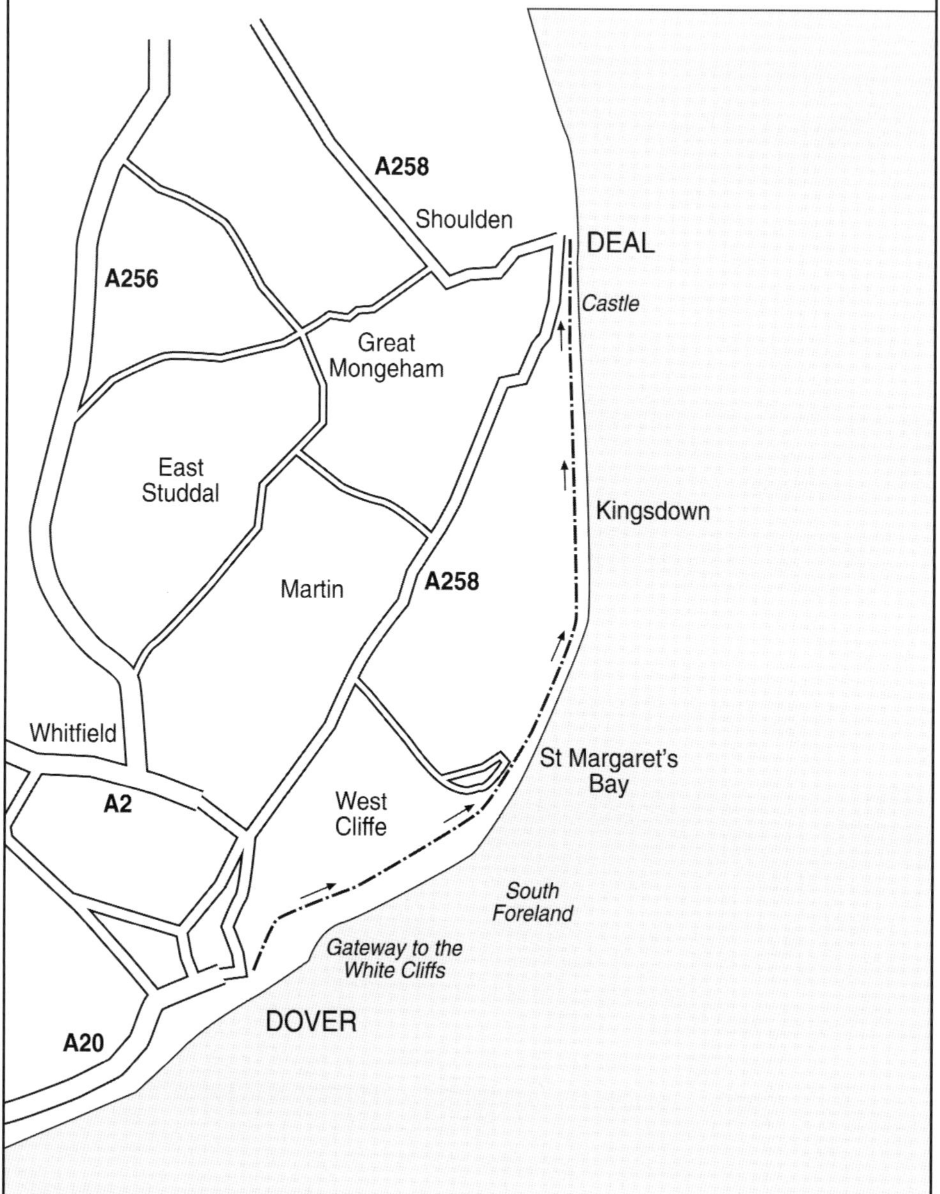

SECTION 3 - **DOVER TO DEAL**

Distance:	10 miles.
Route:	Dover - East Cliff - St Margaret's Bay - Kingsdown - Walmer - Deal.
Maps:	OS Explorer Sheets 138, 150.
Public Transport:	Regular train services from Dover to London Charing Cross via Folkestone, and from Dover to London Victoria via Faversham. Regular train services from Deal to Dover, Sandwich and Ramsgate.
Conditions:	Although this lacks the drama of the previous section, there is some excellent cliff walking, there are good paths and promenades almost throughout, and at journey's end there are two superb castles and a most attractive town.
Refreshments:	See Appendix.

On the assumption that you will have broken your journey to explore Dover, return to the waterfront where you left it, and continue north-eastwards along the waterfront until you reach the Premier Travel inn. Just beyond the inn bear left to a pedestrian crossing over the A20, cross over the road and join the East Cliff road immediately over the other side which proceeds quite sharply uphill, starting as a rather narrow road but quickly opening out. As it opens out you keep to the left, going forward past Athol Terrace to join a path which now again goes fairly steeply uphill, with some sections of steps. Ignoring turnings off or parallel paths, continue to climb, passing under a bridge carrying the A2, an extremely busy trunk road which provides a bypass route for traffic leaving the Eastern Docks bound for Ashford and London. You reach the crest of the hill, and as you do so look out for a Saxon Shore Way signpost which points to the right along a grassy path, and turn right here to follow the Saxon Shore Way as indicated. Keeping a car park to your left, simply follow the path and now enjoy a magnificent cliff top walk: this is one of the best sections of the entire Kent coastal walk and a clear day will be a massive advantage. You are now literally on top of the White Cliffs of Dover and looking down at the bustle of the Eastern Docks with its huge variety of shipping and cargo. There are lots of paths to choose from initially - the simplest advice is stick to the one nearest the cliff edge, thus gaining the best views - but as you gain height, the options diminish and you can enjoy a straightforward, very enjoyable, clifftop march with no route-finding dilemmas. Sharing your route not only with the Saxon Shore Way but also the White Cliffs Country Trail, you proceed confidently along the clifftop to South Foreland, which could be described as the most south-easterly point of the British Isles, approximately two and a half miles from the centre of Dover as the crow flies.

As you proceed along the top of the chalk cliffs, some 300ft above the sea, look out for the lighthouse to your left: this is South Foreland lighthouse, built in 1843 to guide sailors past the notorious Goodwin Sands nearby, although a lighthouse was first erected here for the same purpose as long ago as 1634. The lighthouse is owned by the National Trust and on a clear day it is possible to view the coast of France from its parapet. The lighthouse has important associations with the Italian inventor Marconi who in 1898 made history by sending a message in Morse code from here to a ship twelve miles offshore, and three months later succeeded in sending a wireless signal from South Foreland across the Channel to France. Having passed the lighthouse, turn left, as directed by a Saxon Shore Way signpost, away from the cliff edge. Soon, however, the fence to your right ends, enabling you to turn right and very shortly right again on to a rough driveway. Follow the driveway past some residential properties, heading for a windmill: this is a fine weather-boarded smock mill, the last smock mill to be built in Kent, constructed as recently as 1928/9 in order to generate electricity. Continue along the driveway to the left of the windmill, access to which is not possible, then just past the windmill, and beyond the surrounding vegetation, turn right through a gate to resume your cliff-edge walk. There are now lovely views ahead to the village of St Margaret's Bay.

Now you begin to descend to St Margaret's Bay, dropping to a gate where you are forced to turn left, away from the cliff edge. You go down quite steeply along a track, then at the T-junction bear right along Beach Road into the village, passing Pines gardens and the St Margaret's Museum which at the time of writing housed a welcome tearoom. If you have time, you might want to detour inland to St Margaret's at Cliffe to view the 12th century village church of St Margaret, a complete and virtually unaltered Norman church with a magnificent and richly carved west door, and a really impressive interior that includes splendid arcading along the nave. The church was shelled twice during World War 2 and contains a stained-glass memorial to the victims of the Zeebrugge ferry disaster. Back on the route, continue on past the museum to the next T-junction of tracks where you bear right again, almost immediately arriving at a road on a sharp bend beside South Sands House. Turn right on to the road and drop down to the shore, passing the Coast Guard inn, which boasts that it is closer to France than any other pub in Britain! You are back at sea level for the first time since leaving Dover, and if it is a hot day you may well feel tempted to dip your toes into the waters of St Margaret's Bay. The authors Ian Fleming and Noel Coward both lived here for a time, but of the houses that stood alongside the beach here, most were destroyed by shelling in World War 2. In former times this was a

The statue of Churchill in the beautiful Pines gardens at St Margaret's Bay, with words that seem particularly apposite given the closeness of the Bay to the French coast and the real threat of German invasion in 1940.

popular landing place for smugglers.

Your sojourn along the shore is a short one: you pass through a car parking area, and as you do so you need to watch for and then climb a flight of steps a short way along to the left. At the top, simply continue north-eastwards, passing the picturesquely-named Coney Burrow Point, and climbing gently to find yourself back on the tops of the white cliffs again. Shortly to your left is the magnificent tall granite obelisk memorial to the 1914-1918 Dover Patrol, which played a vital part in the defence of the English shores during World War 1. A similar monument can be found on Cap Blanc Nez just across the English Channel. It is certainly worth detouring the short distance off the coast path to look at "our" obelisk, unveiled in July 1921, before continuing along the clear clifftop path passing Hope Point. You have turned the corner, as it were, and are now following an east-facing coastline, enjoying magnificent, very easy walking; just take care not to stray too close to the cliff edge as there is no fence. To your left is rolling, cultivated downland, and between you and the cliff edge may be found guelder rose, gorse and sweetbriar. You pass the Walmer & Kingsdown Golf Club which is to your left, and soon you are enjoying splendid views towards Kingsdown, Walmer, Deal and Sandwich Bay, with the North Foreland peninsula beyond; on a clear day it may be possible to identify the coastline of France.

Now you begin to descend, passing houses that are situated to your left.
After so many miles of terrific walking and so many interesting things to see, the next piece of the route is something of an anticlimax, as the path drops down to sea level at Oldstairs Bay to arrive at Undercliff Road. Maintaining the same direction, you follow the road, keeping the shingle to your right, but when the road bends to the left, turn right on to the shingle and strike out across it, aiming just to the right of the Zetland Arms pub which, with its conspicuous sign, you can see straight ahead. This is the toughest walking of this section, even tougher than the climbs out of Dover and St Margaret's Bay! Soon you arrive at a concrete promenade, which you now follow, keeping the sea to your right; it is a relief to be off the shingle, but the relief is short lived, for beyond the pub the promenade peters out and you are back on the shingle again. The straggly village of Kingsdown is to your left. Unless you require the amenities offered by the village, it really is not worth detouring into its centre: whilst it has a few pleasant cottages, some built from flint, stone and salvaged ships' timbers, Keith Spence writes that the village is "faceless" and Pevsner describes the village church of St John the Evangelist, built in 1850, as "very dreadful!" The Royal Marines, who were based in neighbouring Deal until 1996, had firing ranges near Kingsdown. Previously a busy centre for smuggling, it once supported a flourishing fishing community, providing large quantities of fish to London and elsewhere, and there was a lifeboat based here from 1866 until 1927.

The White Cliffs of Dover, immortalised in song by Vera Lynn, extend some way both east and west of that town. This is the view of the cliffs at St Margaret's Bay from just below the Dover Patrol memorial to the north-east of the Bay.

Beyond the concrete promenade mentioned above, you continue along the shingle. You could simply follow this, but for an easier walk, which still gives you a sense of a true coastal tramp, look out on your left shortly for Boundary Road which approaches from the left; head for this road as it meets the beach and forms a junction with Wellington Parade which runs north from Boundary Road. It is a rather grandiose name for a somewhat nondescript residential road, but Wellington Parade does at least give easy shingle-free walking which gets even better as it turns into a pedestrian/cycle track. Now the going becomes really straightforward as well as pleasurable, your track going forward to the main historic highlight of this section, namely the stone-built Walmer Castle, which is just to your left across the coast road.

Walmer Castle and Village

Walmer was the most southerly of a trio of castles built for Henry VIII in 1539, neighbouring Deal and Sandown being the others, whose purpose was to protect the so-called Downs roadstead; the Downs roadstead was an area of safe anchorage between the shore and the infamous Goodwin Sands, dangerous sandbanks lying 6 miles out to sea, exposed at low tide and notorious for shipwrecks. These three castles were among many fortifications built on the Channel coast around that time, resulting from Henry VIII's fear of invasion by Catholic France after the English Reformation. Walmer Castle, the most impressive features of which are the gun-ports on the seaward side, is now the official residence of the Lord Warden of the Cinque Ports, having been converted for living in approximately 1730 by the Duke of Dorset and extended in the mid 19th century. As Keith Spence points out, with its Georgian rooms, picture windows and landscape gardens "it is more of a country house than a bastion of coastal defence." One of the Lords Warden was the Duke of Wellington, and the room in the castle where he died in 1852 has been left virtually unaltered since that time; in the next room lie a pair of original Wellington Boots. The gardens were designed by Lady Hester Stanhope, niece of another Lord Warden, William Pitt the Younger, and in 1997 a walled garden was created here by English Heritage in honour of the late Queen Mother, who also held the office of Lord Warden. Walmer itself, reputed landing place of Julius Caesar in 55 BC, is now in reality a suburb of Deal, but boasts a church (St Mary's in Church Street, well inland of the castle) with Norman features, and in the adjoining churchyard there are the ruins of Walmer Court, a Norman semi-fortified house. On the green in Walmer stands the Deal Memorial Bandstand which commemorates eleven Royal Marine bandsmen killed by an IRA bomb at the Royal Marines School of Music, Deal, in 1989.

Having detoured to visit Walmer Castle, continue along the pedestrian/cycle track towards Deal. Look out, however, for a signed footway bearing off to the right by a fine greensward, enabling you to continue your coastal walk on a path that is closer to the seafront. Soon you are on a proper promenade which passes the eastern edge of Walmer and continues on to Deal with which, as stated above, Walmer is joined. You pass right beside the castle (about which more below) and keep going until you arrive at the pier, from which it is a very short walk to the town's amenities and other buildings of interest. The centre of the town is equally accessible from the inland side of the castle.

Deal

Deal is a bustling town, and one of just two coastal towns in Kent - Broadstairs being the other - to face east (Leysdown-on-Sea, on the Isle of Sheppey, also faces east but although it is a busy holiday centre it could hardly be called a town!). The original village was situated inland and is now known as Upper Deal. It was only during the 17th century that the coastal town started to develop from the fisherman's huts on the beach hereabouts, and gradually evolved to form what Pevsner describes as a "17th century new town." By the mid-19th century the development had reached the old village and the town took on the shape that it has today. Although it boasts a pier, and Pevsner remarks on its "mammoth" Queens Hotel, it has never acquired the same fame as a seaside resort that is enjoyed by its near neighbours Broadstairs or Margate, nor has it developed as a port like Dover or Ramsgate, although it counts fishing and boatbuilding as well as tourism amongst its industries. The pier has always been particularly popular with fishermen, with catches regularly including bass, cod, dogfish, flounder, mullet, plaice and sole.

Unquestionably the most impressive historic building in Deal is its castle. What makes it particularly interesting is its unique circular form, with a central keep that is surrounded by two rings of half a dozen semi-circular bastions; the internal layout of the castle has survived almost intact, but all bar one of the original battlements have gone, the flimsy battlements on the keep dating only from 1732. The castle is also noteworthy for the number of gunports,

Deal Castle, one of three castles built in the locality by Henry VIII to protect local shipping, damaged during World War 2 and now impressively restored.

curved bastions for cannonballs to bounce off, ornate gateway, and massive outer walls. It suffered bomb damage during World War 2 but has been restored as near as possible to how it would have looked in the mid 17th century, and in the keep there is a very good exhibition showing how coastal defences have evolved since Roman times. The castle is now owned by English Heritage.

The Time Ball tower close to the sea front at Deal which for over 70 years gave the time to shipping that was anchored offshore. It is now one of the town's most conspicuous and distinctive landmarks.

Other fine secular buildings in Deal include the very prominent Time Ball Tower, which between 1855 and 1927 gave the time to shipping anchored offshore; the barracks near the castle that were built for the Royal Marines in 1795 and which until comparatively recently housed the Royal Marines School Of Music; the yellow brick Town Hall in the High Street, built in 1803, perched on Tuscan columns and constructed at an angle to the street; the extravagantly gabled Post Office in Stanhope Road, built around 1904 and described by Pevsner as a "jolly affair;" and the Maritime and Local History Museum with some fascinating old boats among its exhibits. The original iron pier was opened in 1864 but it was badly damaged in World War 2 and the present pier was opened as recently as 1957. Of the churches in Deal, the most interesting are St Leonard's in the Upper Deal area, half a mile inland, Norman in origin and with a fine red-brick battlemented west tower dating from 1684, and the red-brick St George's in the High Street, built at the start of the 18th century. William Cobbett was less than impressed with Deal, calling it a "villainous place, full of filthy looking people."

SECTION 4 - **DEAL TO RAMSGATE**

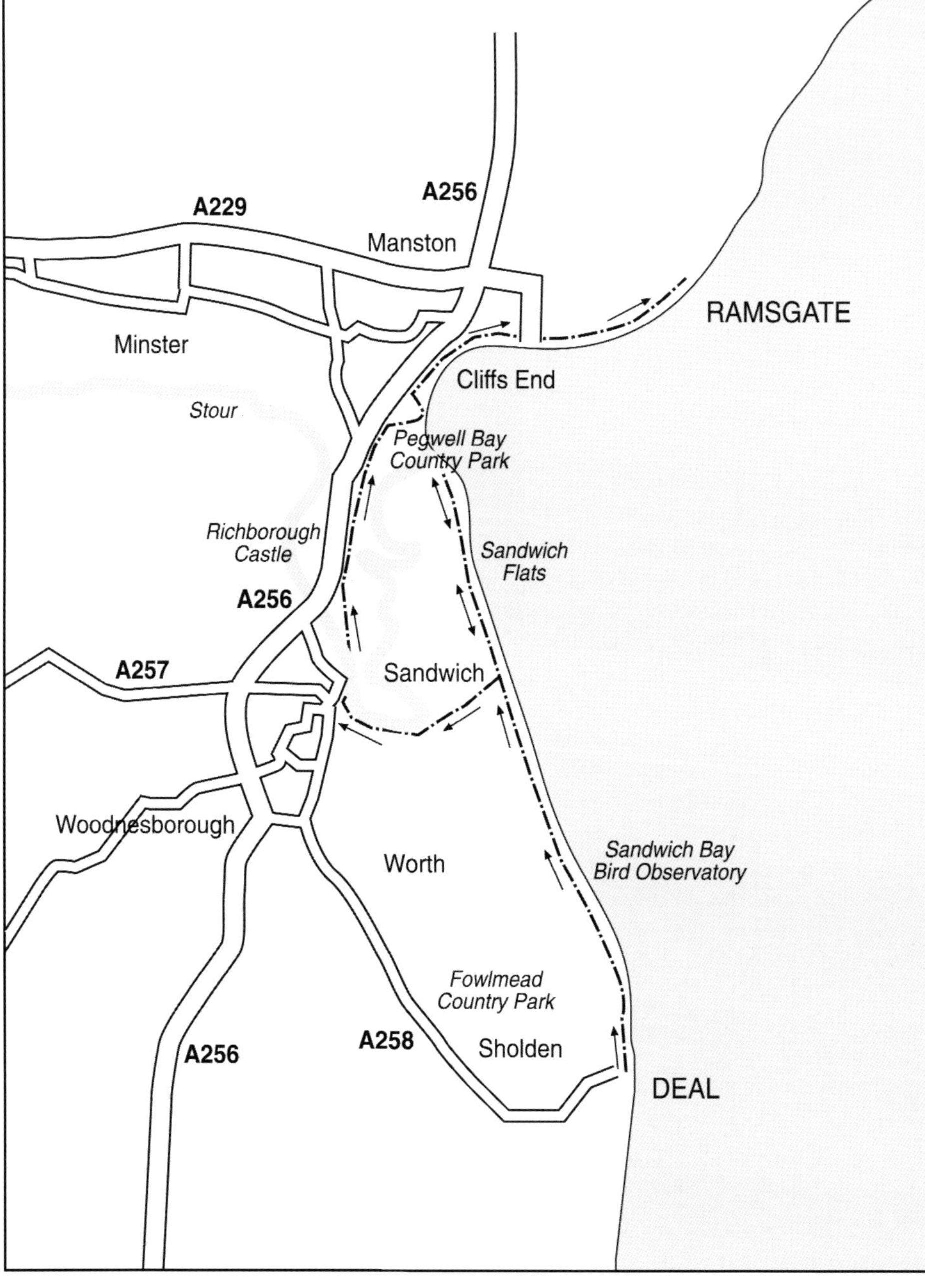

SECTION 4 - **DEAL TO RAMSGATE**

Distance:	10 miles (direct route); 3 extra miles for Stour mouth detour; 4 extra miles for Richborough Castle detour.
Route:	Deal - Cinque Ports Golf Club - Royal St George's Golf Club - Prince's Golf Club - mouth of Stour (optional) - Sandwich - Richborough Castle(optional) - Sandwich - Richborough - Pegwell Bay - Ramsgate.
Map:	OS Explorer Sheet 150.
Public Transport:	Regular train service linking Deal, Sandwich and Ramsgate, with excellent connecting service from Ramsgate to London Victoria via Faversham. There are trains also from Deal to Dover with connections to London Victoria and Charing Cross.
Conditions:	This is pleasant rather than spectacular walking with very little cliff scenery. There is a most tiresome piece of roadwalking to negotiate the Stour, but there are compensations in Sandwich, the loveliest town on the route. There are two lengthy optional detours which could add up to 7 extra miles to this section; as the next section is only 8 miles long, you might in those circumstances decide to end this section at Sandwich instead.
Refreshments:	See Appendix.

Leaving the centre of Deal behind, continue along the promenade beyond the pier; the walking remains straightforward and enjoyable but the promenade is noticeably narrower and there is a more suburban feel to the built-up areas to your left. Soon, however, you pull away from the residential sprawl to the north of the town centre and the comforting concrete promenade comes to an end. It is good to be back out in more open country, and you can now enjoy really excellent views across Sandwich Bay to Ramsgate, the end of this section, which looks a deceptively short distance away. As the built-up area and the promenade come to an end, you reach the site of Sandown Castle, the first and most northerly of the trio of castles in the Deal area that were built to protect shipping that sought anchorage in the Downs roadstead. Built, like its neighbours, around 1539/1540, its original plan was almost identical to that of Walmer, but over time it succumbed to the sea and all that is left is a fragment of the tunnel-vaulted basement on the shore, appearing as barely more than a heap of stones. Although the firm promenade is left behind, a coast path continues in the form of a rougher stony track. You have Sandwich Bay and views to Ramsgate ahead of you, while to your left is the Royal Cinque Ports Golf Club, the first of three really fine golf courses beside which you will walk in the next three miles or so; beyond the golf courses are the massive funnels of the Richborough power station and the big industrial works at Great Stonar. These ugly buildings will remain more or less constant features of the landscape for virtually the whole of the rest of this section. Royal Cinque Ports Golf Club, also known as Deal Golf Club, has been a championship golf course of international repute; the British Open was held here in 1909 and 1920 and to this day it hosts the Halford Hewitt, a knock-out competition between public school teams from across the country. Continue along the trusty track - a pub is signposted a short way off the path to the left - and go forward to a curious assembly of buildings known as the Sandwich Bay Estate. The estate belonged to the Earl of Guilford who began to develop it around 1912, and a number of architects, contemporaries of the great Sir Edwin Lutyens, accepted commissions for big houses between the Cinque Ports golf links and the Royal St George's golf links, about which more below. The architects, among them Sir Reginald Blomfield, Paul Phipps and Bailey Scott & Beresford, adopted what were fashionable styles for the building, including neo-Queen Anne, and a version of Lutyens' butterfly-shaped house, Papillon Hall. These imposing and quite exotic buildings look somewhat incongruous in the context of the surroundings, Spence describing the estate as "a Millionaire's Row stuck down here in opulent isolation."

As you reach the estate you will find the stony track is replaced by a concrete drive which does make for faster walking, and you can now make really rapid progress beside Sandwich Bay. The bay itself has always been famous for migrant birds, and a bird observatory was established here in 1961; the best time to visit is autumn, when departing warblers and flycatchers mingle with arriving finches and thrushes, while the end of October sees the visit of Pallas' warblers from Siberia. In the spring you may find a variety of orchids, such as southern marsh and pyramidal, on the dunes and in the roughs of the nearby golf courses, and there are some rare flora to be found here including sea holly and yellow rattle. Now continuing beyond the estate, you will see to your left the fairways, tees, greens, bunkers and sandhills of Royal St George's, one of the most famous golf courses in the world. Founded in 1887, it became in 1894 the first golf course outside Scotland to host the British Open Golf Championship, and since then it has hosted the Championship a further twelve times, the most recent occasion (at the time of writing) being 2003 when the tournament was won by a little-known American, Ben Curtis; previous winners here have included the great British golfers J.H. Taylor, Harry Vardon and Henry Cotton. The British Amateur

Championship has also been played here on a number of occasions. The course features strongly in the James Bond film *Goldfinger,* based on the novel by Ian Fleming, himself a club member; in the film, Bond successfully takes on the eponymous villain in a match here for $10,000.

Continuing along the concrete path - you could walk along the shingle if you preferred but you gain no better views - you arrive at a large blue signboard advertising the third golf course, Prince's. This, too, has hosted the British Open Championship, albeit only once, in 1932, when the American Gene Sarazen was the winner. The course has been greatly altered following its use during World War 2 as a battle training area; the famous Battle of Britain pilot Laddie Lucas was born in the original Prince's clubhouse and when in trouble during one air battle he was able to use his local knowledge to land his damaged Spitfire on the golf course. As you reach the blue signboard, a decision has to be taken. Ahead is the natural barrier of the river Stour, and not only is there no way across it, but it is impossible to follow the bank from its mouth to the first upstream crossing in the town of Sandwich. The continuous coastal route must therefore leave the shoreline here, proceeding a little farther along the track towards an old boarded-up golf clubhouse, then turning left to follow the Stour Valley Walk along a clear path towards Sandwich. The path shortly seems to fizzle out into a grassy area, but the right of way simply continues across the grass in the same direction, aiming for a Stour Valley Walk signpost, from which the path is clear once more. Follow the path to a T-junction with a road, turning left on to the road then almost immediately right on to a metalled path* that goes beside the Stour all the way into Sandwich.

If you have sufficient time and energy, however, you may wish to follow the shoreline as far as the mouth of the Stour and effectively the point where Sandwich Bay meets the more substantial inlet of Pegwell Bay, on the northern side of which stands the town of Ramsgate. It is possible to turn right off the concrete track by the blue signboard mentioned above to join a clear path beside the shore which continues for a mile and a half to the mouth of the Stour. The path is initially well defined and easy to follow, but as you make progress further north, passing the new Prince's clubhouse, the going tends to get rougher; you may well find it more agreeable to walk along the sand, which is generally firm, although there are softer patches, which provide rather more difficult walking. There are excellent views across Pegwell Bay to Ramsgate, while to your left are the huge cooling towers of the Richborough power station. In due course, as you draw level with the power station, tall posts marking the course of the Stour come into view ahead of you, but take immense care as you approach the river, for the sand gets noticeably softer and gooier with each step, and you may decide to stop a little short of the water to avoid the risk of getting your shoes or even your legs stuck. There is no bridge, and no riverside path to Sandwich (don't even think about wading across!!), so frustratingly you are forced back on yourself. Although you do not have to go quite all the way back to the blue signboard mentioned above you must still retrace your steps, proceeding along the sand or the path, according to choice, until you draw level with the new Prince's clubhouse. A little way beyond that, look out to your right for an isolated conifer tree, just past which there is a stile in the fence to your right; use the path through the dunes to go up to and cross this stile, then go forward to the Prince's clubhouse approach road and walk straight across it, to join a clear track on the other side. Now follow this track across the golf course, taking care to watch for low-flying golf balls! Once beyond the golf course, keep going along the track which passes some storage buildings and enters cultivated land, in due course arriving at a stile and, immediately beyond it, a T-junction with a wider track. Turn left on to this track and follow it. The track soon becomes a proper metalled road which runs dead straight for a few hundred yards, then bends sharply left; at this left-hand bend turn right on to the metalled path marked with an asterisk* above. You are now back on the continuous route.

Now it is just a short walk along the metalled path to Sandwich, keeping the Stour close by to your right. The buildings of the town do not come into view immediately and there is a lovely pastoral feel about this part of the walk which contrasts quite radically with the shoreline walking completed earlier in this section. You use a footbridge to cross a subsidiary channel then shortly turn right along a combined footpath/cycleway, a very popular amenity for Sandwich townsfolk and visitors. The path proceeds unerringly to the all-important river bridge crossing, but if you wish you can follow the greensward separating the path from the river; to continue on towards Ramsgate you turn right to cross the bridge, but Sandwich, with its wealth of lovely buildings and amenities, is just a short distance to the left, on the same side of the river. You would have to be in a tearing hurry to bypass it! (NOTE: Should you wish to visit the remains of the 3rd century Richborough Castle - see below - you will need to leave the coast path at Sandwich and follow the Saxon Shore Way, which leaves our coast route here, out of Sandwich westwards via Strand Street and The Causeway and along the left(west) bank of the Stour. Having visited the castle, you will then need to retrace your steps all the way to Sandwich. It is a lengthy detour, with no coastal walking, and, especially if you have followed the longer route from Deal as described above, you may have difficulty in completing the whole of the Deal-Ramsgate section in a day incorporating the detour.)

Sandwich

Though it stands well inland today, this town was in fact situated on the coast during the Anglo-Saxon period and into the early Middle Ages, and developed into one of the most important ports in England as well as becoming one of the five original Cinque Ports. It was via Sandwich that Thomas a Becket fled to France and later returned to martyrdom at Canterbury, and at Sandwich that Richard I landed on his return from the Crusades. Its prestige peaked in the early 13th century: in 1217 the boy king Henry III defeated the French in the Battle of Sandwich, a sea battle at nearby Pegwell Bay. The port was subjected to heavy

The streets of Sandwich are dotted with attractive independent shops, one of which is its popular bookshop. Note the beautifully preserved sign above the shop windows indicating the previous usage of the premises.

raids by the French in the 15th century causing very considerable damage, then during the 16th century the silting of the Stour caused the sea to recede and the days of Sandwich as a port were over. It now presents as a town of contrasts: the central and older part and also the quay area have an endearing chocolate box quality, seemingly deriving most of its income from the tourist trade, but the town has a number of thriving industries, especially pharmaceutical research, with a massive industrial complex to the north.

The centre of Sandwich is a maze of narrow streets with many very attractive brick and painted town houses, several dating back to the 18th century. There is no one central street or focal point of note, the historic buildings being dotted around High Street, St Peter Street, King Street, Delf Street and New Street: indeed despite the small size of the town centre, it is surprisingly easy to lose one's bearings when walking around the town. Among the grandest buildings in Sandwich are the gates, namely the Barbican which was built in 1539 and the medieval Fisher Gate built in 1384, and the Guildhall which dates from 1579 with its old courtroom, council chamber and museum. The principal church of Sandwich, St Clement's in Knightrider Street, now the town's parish church, has a huge Norman tower that dates back to around 1100, a 15th century octagonal font carved with various heraldic shields which include the arms of the Cinque Ports, and a system of sounding holes below the choir stalls and high on the sanctuary walls to form a kind of medieval amplification. The two other medieval churches of the town are shadows of their former selves. St Mary's in Strand Street,

Sandwich in festive mood. Rising splendidly above the picturesque narrow streets of the town is the huge Norman tower of the church of St Clement.

dating from the 12th century, is partially ruined, the central tower having fallen in in 1668 although remnants of the original survive, while St Peter's, dating from the late 13th century, lost its tower in 1661 and latterly has served as a tourist information office. Other outstanding buildings in Sandwich include the fine timbered Sandwich Weavers in Strand Street, the name Weavers recalling the days when the town was the centre of the immigrant Flemish weaving industry; the timbered Old House, also in Strand Street, where Queen Elizabeth I is believed to have stayed when she visited the town in 1573; the 1592 King's Arms, also in Strand Street, described by Pevsner as "the best timber-framed house in Sandwich;" the fine 16th century brick Manwood Court, again in Strand Street, built originally as a school; the early 18th century Congregational Chapel, its roof supported by 2 masts from ships used by French Protestant refugees; and the Victorian almshouses and 13th century chapel making up the present St Bartholomew's Hospital which was founded around the beginning of the 13th century. Two more recent buildings of note are the huge red-brick Queen Anne style Bell Hotel which overshadows the Barbican, and, again in neo-Queen Anne style, the Salutation at the end of Upper Strand Street, designed by Sir Edwin Lutyens. Its mature garden, laid out by Lutyens in collaboration with Gertrude Jekyll, is particularly attractive.

The town's name has been immortalised in an edible context, thanks to John Montagu (1718-1792), the fourth holder of the title of Earl of Sandwich. He was First Lord of the Admiralty three times but although he sponsored Captain Cook's voyages of discovery, he was notorious for his ineptitude and his corruptness. He was also prone to gambling, and so that he might remain at the gaming tables without interruption (sources kinder to him suggest it was so that he could spend longer in his office) he had convenience meals prepared for him, one of the most successful of which was a slice of cold roast beef between two pieces of toast. The term "sandwich" for such a meal has stuck ever since.

Having crossed the bridge over the Stour, you are now in the part of Kent known as the Isle of Thanet. The name of Thanet is thought to be of Celtic origin and meaning "bright island;" in Roman and Saxon times Thanet really was an island, being cut off from the mainland by the rivers Stour and Wantsum. It can easily be identified on maps of Kent as the piece of the county forming the promontory at its north eastern tip, edged with chalk cliffs, and containing the seaside towns of Ramsgate, Broadstairs and Margate with Pegwell Bay to its south, and, as stated above, the rivers Stour and Wantsum effectively forming its border with the rest of Kent. Your arrival in Thanet is hardly distinguished, for you are now faced with a long dull walk back to the sea from Sandwich, although you may be consoled to learn that there is nothing as uninspiring as this to come for a good 40 miles or more. Continue along the road in the same direction, passing initially suburban housing and then a massive industrial complex including the huge works of the Pfizer company, among whose products is Viagra. Keep along the road until its end, then bear right to follow alongside the A256 Dover-Ramsgate road; there is a pedestrian/cycle path to the right of the road, so the walking is at least safe, but it is not pretty, especially as you are now right in the shadow of the cooling towers of Richborough power station, which was completed in 1963 but is now disused. The land to the right of the road at this point is marked on maps as Richborough Port, a reminder of the days when Richborough was on the coast and, in 43 AD, the chief port of the Romans' entry into Britain, with the Roman name Rutupiae. The original port became marooned in salt marshes but a transport depot was established here in 1916 and the area was used as an embarkation point for the D-day invasion. Sadly the chief glory of Richborough, its castle which was in fact a Roman fort built in the 3rd century to defend the port and of which some of the 12 ft thick walls still remain, is across the Stour and there is no chance of gaining access to it from here; to do so you would have needed to follow the Saxon Shore Way north-westwards from Sandwich on the western side of the river as described above.

Having passed the towers of the power station, you plod on, with no noticeable improvement in your surroundings, the only redeeming feature being a service station to your right which may provide some well-earned refreshment. Now watch out for a road forking off left to Stonelees golf club. Pass this left fork, keeping on the right(east) side of the main road, then very shortly beyond the fork your path becomes separated from the road by vegetation; in a few hundred yards you leave the path, turning right on to a wide clearly-defined path that takes you eastwards to within sight of Pegwell Bay and Ramsgate. Your long detour away from the coast proper is over. It is grand to be back by the sea, which will be within your sight virtually all the way round to beyond Seasalter a good 40 miles distant, but galling to think how much walking has been necessary to negotiate a river just a few feet wide. You are only just now level with the mouth of the Stour and may feel that although Sandwich provided some compensation for the extra miles, a judiciously-placed footbridge or ferry would have been even more acceptable!

Now the going is straightforward and enjoyable, with a delightful path quite close to the shore looking out onto Pegwell Bay; rejoicing in this rather unusual name, thought to mean "well or spring where pigs drink," the bay has been a magnet for continental invaders, including not only the Romans but the Saxons and the Vikings too. Today it is a peaceful place and a nature lover's paradise, and with its mixture of sand dunes, saltmarsh and tidal mudflats, it boasts a profusion of plant life including wild asparagus and sea holly. It is a breeding ground for ringed plovers and little terns, and in summer one may observe migrant butterflies here such as the clouded yellow and painted lady. I had the good fortune to walk this section very early on an August morning and was able to watch the sun rise across the bay, a quite unforgettable sight. You soon find yourself heading back towards the A256 and a rather unsightly petrol station; pass to the right of this and climb up to a greensward giving not only a grandstand view of Pegwell Bay but also a chance to view the magnificent replica Viking ship Hugin with its dragon's head and rows of shields on each side. In 1949, in commemoration of the 1500th anniversary of the landing at nearby Ebbsfleet of Hengista and Horsa, the first Anglo Saxon settlers in Britain, a Danish crew re-enacted their crossing of the Channel, using this very ship. At the far corner of the greensward join a path that now proceeds along a cliff top; it is your first piece of cliff walking since your descent to Kingsdown south of Deal and feels quite exhilarating after so much tramping along the flat, with super views across Pegwell Bay extending right down past Deal towards South Foreland. St Augustine, sent by the Pope to convert England to Christianity,

The replica Viking ship Hugin, used by a Danish crew in 1949 to re-enact the crossing of the Channel by Hengista and Horsa, the first Anglo Saxon settlers in Britain, 1500 years previously.

landed hereabouts in 597 AD and a St Augustine cross and well can be found at Cliffsend, where he is said to have met King Ethelbert.

All too soon your clifftop march ends, the footpath passing some coastguard cottages and arriving at a road junction. Turn right to follow Pegwell Road eastwards then slightly north of east, moving a little away from the shore with a caravan park to your right. Look out for Goodwin Road leading off to the left; directly opposite the Goodwin Road turning is a right-hand turn, effectively a walkway leading seawards again, and shortly you arrive at what is the western end of the Royal Esplanade. Turn left and now enjoy a delightful high-level promenade beside the Esplanade which will bring you to the bustling and sprawling town of Ramsgate. To your right, and below, is the Royal Harbour Approach leading to Ramsgate's busy ferry port - you will enjoy an excellent view of large ferries arriving at or leaving the port - and soon you will see the imposing Regency Hotel to your left, a sad sight with many windows boarded up at the time of writing. Beyond the hotel, your walkway now descends to harbour level; pause before you descend and enjoy the superb view of the harbour and marina with its profusion of boats and a backcloth of old houses and shops. Then make your way downhill to arrive at the water's edge, with the marina immediately to the right. This section of the walk ends here, with the amenities of the town including shops and buses within easy reach; the railway station is unfortunately set well back from the sea, in the St Lawrence area of the town, so make sure you allow time for the extra walk or bus ride if you are catching a train onwards from here.

Ramsgate

Ramsgate, translated from "Hroefngeat," meaning "raven's gap," is a combination of seaside resort and busy cross-Channel port, and is a centre for yachting and fishing. It was once one of the Cinque Ports, although not one of the original five; the harbour was completed in 1763 and extended in 1818, and it developed as a holiday town in the 19th century after being popularised by a visit from George IV in 1827. The King is commemorated in the form of an obelisk that was put up in 1822 to mark a voyage he made to Hanover, and subsequently he granted the harbour Royal status. It was always regarded as somewhat superior to its neighbour Margate, the Chambers Journal of 1853 referring to its "stuckuppishness and stiff and formal society;" the Ramsgate sands, which incidentally has been rhyming slang for "hands," were described by C.E. Pascoe in 1886 as "a rendezvous of Punch and Judy men, nigger minstrels, donkey drivers and the like." A pier was erected in 1881, stretching for 555ft and boasting a scenic railway, and was demolished in 1931. The town is perhaps more famous now as a ferry port than as a resort; in 1969 the hoverport was opened for passenger and vehicle conveyance to Calais in France, with a cross-Channel terminal opening in 1981. Both Ostend, in Belgium, and Dunkirk, in France, have been served in recent years by ferries operating from the port, although all hovercraft crossings were subsequently moved to Dover. A number of influential figures have been drawn to, or had connections with, the town. The architect Augustus Pugin built a house for himself in Ramsgate in the 1840's and also designed the Roman Catholic church which is dedicated, appropriately enough, to St Augustine; the poet Samuel Taylor Coleridge was a regular visitor in summer in the early 19th century; the novelist R.M. Ballantyne researched some of his stories here; the broadcaster Frank Muir and the philosopher A.N. Whitehead were both born in the town; Karl Marx, the founder of Communism, is known to have stayed in the town; in the 1870's Vincent van Gogh lived at 6 Royal Road in the town, working as a language master before making his career in painting; and Jane Austen's brother Frank was stationed here. She herself visited the town in around 1803 and used it as a setting for Wickham's attempt to elope with Darcy's sister in her famous novel Pride And Prejudice.

The harbour is a particularly appealing feature of the town, Keith Spence going as far as to say it has the nicest harbour in either Kent or Sussex "with two good piers to walk along, an outer harbour with fishing boats pottering about, and an inner harbour with a marina for small craft and wharves where moderate-sized boats unload their cargoes." The yacht marina was opened in 1965, with capacity for 120 boats. There are a number of impressive buildings in the town, with perhaps the most interesting sacred building being the Roman Catholic church in St Augustine's Road, designed, as stated above, by Pugin. His idea was to construct a typical parish church of the Middle Ages, and the resulting interior is described by Pevsner as a "marvel, movingly strong of structure and profuse in the decoration everywhere." Particular features of interest are the brass tabernacle on the high altar, four of Pugin's screens, the carved altar and Pugin memorial in the south transept, and the huge font. The house which Pugin built for himself, called The Grange, is just over the churchyard wall, its main feature being a battlemented south-east tower from which Pugin watched for boats in difficulty in bad weather. Other buildings worth seeing in Ramsgate include the early 19th century Clock House, now a fine maritime museum with lifeboat models, relics of wrecks from the Goodwin Sands, and seafaring memorabilia including navigational instruments (a north-south meridian line on the house's upper floor provided Ramsgate Mean Time, used by Channel ship captains before the advent of GMT); the parish church of St Laurence, dating back to pre-Norman times and containing huge Norman arches and pillars; the Royal Victorian Pavilion, which opened in 1904 and is endowed with what Pevsner describes as a "curvaceous Frenchy roof, channelled rustication, Greek Doric columns and rustic sculpture;" and a number of noteworthy terraces that were built as Ramsgate developed as a seaside resort in the early 19th century, including Nelson Crescent, built between 1798 and 1801, and which, with its continuation the Paragon, include four-storied yellow brick terraces with balconies. The best of the early 19th century terraces is arguably Wellington Crescent, which dates from 1819, with yellow brick and a continuous Greek Doric colonnade.

Two further views of the beautiful little town of Sandwich, which despite having a chocolate-box quality remains a busy workaday place.

SECTION 5 - **RAMSGATE TO MARGATE**

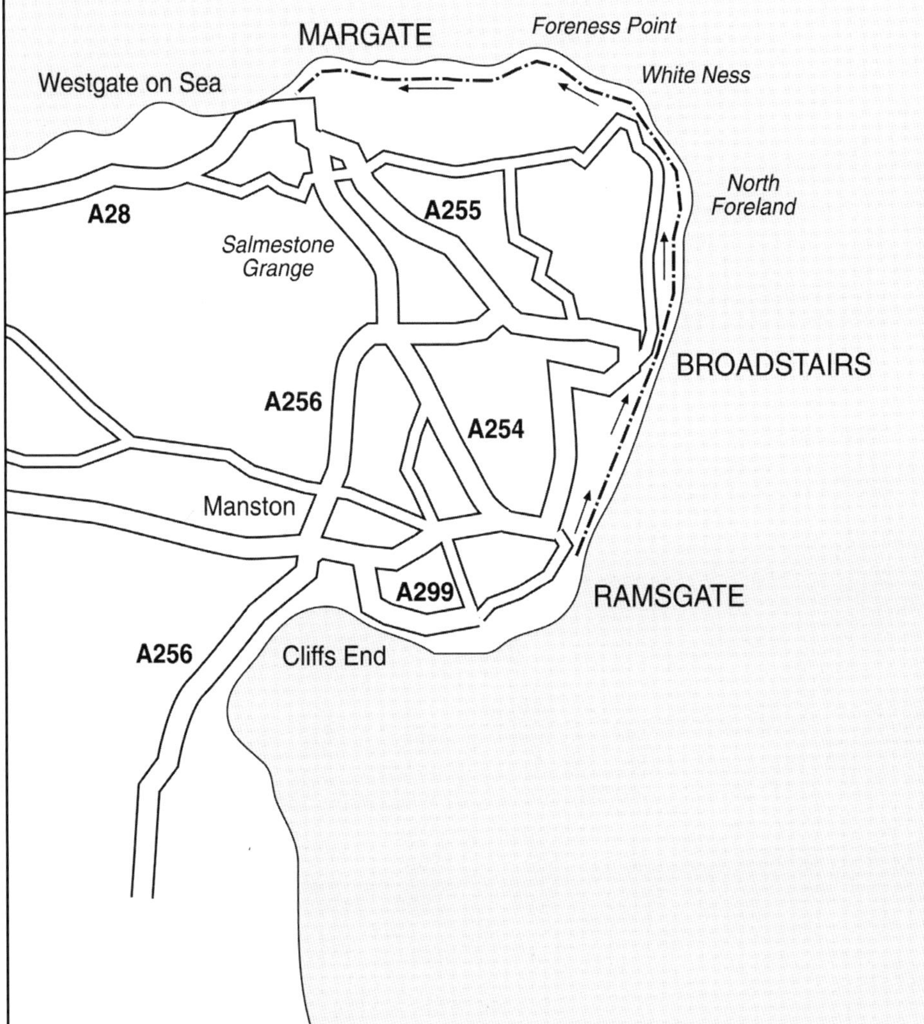

SECTION 5 - **RAMSGATE TO MARGATE**

Distance:	8 miles.
Route:	Ramsgate - Dumpton Point - Broadstairs - North Foreland - Kingsgate - Cliftonville - Margate.
Map:	OS Explorer Sheet 150.
Public Transport:	Excellent train service between Ramsgate and London Victoria via Broadstairs and Margate (two trains an hour most days).
Conditions:	This is good fast walking on a well-defined route with no difficulties whatsoever. Its shortness reflects the fact that you will want to spend time in Ramsgate and Broadstairs, both very interesting towns, and enjoy a pint at the Captain Digby Inn. As intimated in the previous section, you could consider stopping over in Sandwich and walking from there to Margate in one day, especially if you have followed the two optional detours set out in the previous section.
Refreshments:	See Appendix.

Having reached the harbour level at Ramsgate, keep along the road by the water's edge, passing the splendid Queen's Head pub which is on your left, and the somewhat garish Grosvenor Casino to your right. The road bends left and the prospect immediately changes: the picturesque harbour, marina and port are now behind you, while to your right now are the sands and to the left a sheer concrete face on the top of which is built Victoria Parade, providing a high level scenic promenade and the continuation of your journey. To access it, look out for a flight of steep steps cut into the concrete face immediately to your left across Marina Esplanade and Marina Road and climb them to the very top, then having done so, turn right to follow Victoria Parade. Enjoy a last look back at Pegwell Bay then proceed resolutely north-eastwards, passing pretty rock gardens and a belvedere which has sadly been spoilt by graffiti; proceeding in the same direction you leave vehicular traffic behind to follow a path along the right hand edge of a greensward, which is separated from the sea by an area of thick vegetation. This relents and you now enjoy a really lovely clifftop walk, with extensive views out to sea. The path descends, then levels out, with buildings visible to the left which include not only residential properties but Gap House School on the landward side of the coast road, South Cliff Parade. Suddenly the bustle of Ramsgate seems a very long way back. You round Dumpton Bay, the most modest of inlets, using a clear path that steers a happy course between the coast road (now Western Esplanade) and the cliff edge, and goes forward to Dumpton Point: this is not the most dramatic Kent coastal feature, but it is certainly worth pausing here to enjoy the view out to sea and to wave goodbye to the ferries as they head out of Ramsgate towards the Continent. Straightforward, easy walking in a northerly direction takes you past Louisa Bay to within sight of the next town, Broadstairs, to which Ramsgate is effectively joined. You are now, and will continue to be for many miles, on the Viking Coastal Trail, a very well signposted cycle/walkway, and if you are in any doubt as to your route between here and Margate, simply follow the Viking Coastal Trail signposts. You begin to lose height and soon find yourself entering the lovely old town of Broadstairs, with excellent views to the little bay and sands below and to your right. Follow the Viking Coastal Trail along the obvious path above the bay to reach a T-junction with Harbour Street; at this point you have the enticing choice of a very short walk down to the sands or up to the centre of Broadstairs which, unless you are in a tearing hurry, you will almost certainly wish to take time out to enjoy.

Broadstairs

There are two explanations for the town's name. One explanation is that it was named after Our Lady of Bradstow, the medieval shrine of whom stands here; the shrine was regarded as so special that ships would lower their topsails as a mark of respect as they passed by. The town was once actually known as "Bradstow." Another school of thought is that the town's name was derived from the wide set of steps that were cut into the white cliffs, probably early in the 15th century, to lead down to the sea. It is these steps that may well have inspired the title of John Buchan's 1915 thriller The Thirty Nine Steps, after he began the book here in 1914; there were originally 78 steps and Buchan was allegedly advised by a friend to halve the number for the title.

The popularity of Broadstairs as a holiday resort started in Regency times and continued through the 19th century, the town acquiring a reputation, which to an extent continues until the present day, for being rather more "up market" than its neighbour Margate. It was certainly seen as a good enough place for the fictional middle-class Pooter family to holiday in George and Weedon Grossmith's Diary Of A Nobody! It possesses a combination of quaintness and charm that is arguably rather greater than that possessed by other Thanet coastal towns; there is what Pevsner describes as a "charmingly tight" little harbour, "embraced," he adds, "by a horseshoe of low chalk cliffs that ring with the squeals of excited children on a sunny summer's day." There are a number of 19th century terraces and cottages standing back from the cliff edge, several pretty shops and cafes, and delightful sea views, but there are few buildings of special historical interest. The principal church of Broadstairs, the Norman church of St Peter, stands well inland in the district known as St Peter's; in the town itself, of note is the flint-built neo-Georgian Windsor Cinema and the late 18th century

The beach at Broadstairs, with its lovely sands, has been a magnet for visitors since Regency times.

Pierremont Hall beside the High Street, while in Albion Street may be found St Mary's Chapel which is built on the shrine of Our Lady of Bradstow mentioned above.

Besides John Buchan and the Grossmiths, Broadstairs has further connections with well known personalities of the past. The late Sir Edward Heath, prime minister between 1970 and 1974, was born in Broadstairs in 1916, and the round-the-world yachtsman Alec Rose lived in the town. However, the town is perhaps best known for its close association with the author Charles Dickens: he had a holiday home here called Fort House, where he spent much time in the 1850's and 1860's, and which was later renamed Bleak House, in turn providing the title for one of his most celebrated works. Dickens loved the house, calling it his "airy nest." During the period 1849-50, while staying in the house, he wrote his novel David Copperfield in which there features a character called Betsey Trotwood, who was modelled on a Miss Mary Strong who lived in a house in Victoria Parade in the town. Broadstairs' association with Dickens led to the creation of a museum of Dickensiana and the establishment of an annual Dickens festival in the town.

To exit Broadstairs, heading now for North Foreland, it is important to follow the Viking Coastal Trail signposts carefully. On reaching the T-junction with Harbour Street, turn left and immediately right into Fort Road, which you follow; the road swings immediately right again, bringing you back within sight of the sea. Turn left now to head northwards, almost immediately passing Bleak House (see above) which is to your left, and continuing along the Viking Coastal Trail. To begin with, the walking northwards from Broadstairs is initially uncomplicated and still very enjoyable, with good walking past East Cliff, but as you reach an area of trees you are forced to turn left, inland, up Park Road and temporarily away from the coast. Permit

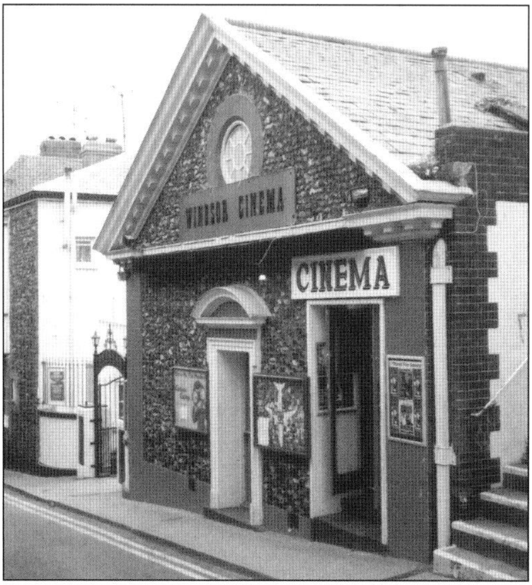

Who says that the video and DVD age have killed the cinema? The beautiful little flint-built neo-Georgian Windsor Cinema at Broadstairs, just a couple of minutes from the beach, is still thriving in the twenty first century.

yourself a smile as you continue along Park Road past Wainwright Court; Alfred Wainwright was of course the doyen of Lakeland walking and his name strikes a chord with walkers everywhere. It is not immediately apparent whether this development was named after him, but he would no doubt be as sad as you are to be temporarily bidding farewell to the invigorating sea air, and trudging into what is a rather nondescript residential area. At the T-junction at the end of Park Road you turn right to proceed up North Foreland Road past modern housing, out of sight of the sea; don't be tempted to follow the shortly-signed footpath which simply goes down to the shore with no possibility of advancement towards North Foreland, but rather continue up North Foreland Road and then turn right along Cliff Road back to the coast.

Now it is a short walk beside the sea to North Foreland, the most north-easterly point of your walk along the coastline of Kent, and you will soon observe the green and white North Foreland lighthouse, with its short thick tower, to your left. Although there has been a lighthouse of sorts here since the early 16th century, the present lighthouse was built late in the 17th century and heightened in 1793, the flint and brick facing being hidden, before being lowered apparently in the late 19th century. In 1998 it became Britain's last lighthouse to be switched to computerised remote control. You will notice the cycle track and Viking Coastal Trail being signposted inland along Crescent Road to pass the lighthouse; unless you want to take a closer look at the lighthouse don't follow the cycle track inland, but rather keep along the cliff path as far as you are able, as far as a car park and a most significant moment on your coastal walk. Ever since you left Camber Sands your predominant direction of travel has been eastwards. However, this is as far to the east as you will go, and as you are forced round to the very conspicuous car park you are now proceeding slightly west of north, with westwards rather than eastwards continuing to be your predominant direction of travel all the way on to the end of the route. Go through the car park and cross the road, known as Joss Gap Road, now reunited with the Viking Coastal Trail;

you turn right and, with Joss Bay to your right, you then follow the roadside path north-westwards, past the splendidly named Hackemdown Point, keeping a golf course immediately to your left, with the sea temporarily out of sight to the right. Continue along the path, still parallel with the road, to arrive at Kingsgate Bay and the remarkable buildings of Kingsgate.

Kingsgate

Taking its name from a gate erected to commemorate the landing of Charles II and his brother in June 1683, Kingsgate is one of the most extraordinary assemblies of buildings you will meet in your pilgrimage around the Thanet coastline. The man responsible was Lord Holland, father of Charles James Fox. A large house known as Holland House, with a giant six-columned Doric portico, was built here in the 1760's for Lord Holland in a hollow close to the cliffs of North Foreland, a location described by Pevsner as "crazy." Lord Holland surrounded it with a host of flint-built follies, not all of which survive. Among them are Port Regis, which became a convent, and which may be reached by following Convent Road briefly south-westwards off the coast road; Hackemdown Tower, built on a Saxon burial mound which Lord Holland excavated in 1765; and Whitfield Tower, built in 1818 in honour of Lord Holland's builder and standing on what is the highest point in Thanet. Horace Walpole thought the combination of house and follies might be mistaken "for a prospect in some half-civilised island discovered by Captain Cook." The most prominent building at Kingsgate today, dating back to 1860, is Kingsgate Castle, the ruined round tower to the south-east of which is the sole remains of Lord Holland's stables. One well known resident of Kingsgate was Jack Warner, who played the title role in the popular BBC police drama Dixon Of Dock Green.

Your walk, still beside the coast road, takes you on past Kingsgate Bay; the cliff scenery here is superb, and includes a natural rock arch reminiscent of Durdle Door on the Dorset coast. Continue the short distance to the Captain Digby Inn which provides a welcome refreshment stop on the otherwise amenity-less walk from Broadstairs to Margate and beside which there is a tremendous view of Kingsgate Castle. Leave the road just past the inn, turning right along a signed path (or taking a short cut through the pub car park if you prefer!) to regain the cliffs; there is a real sense now of turning a corner, a process that began at the car park near the North Foreland lighthouse, and your direction of travel is more decisively westward. Look out hereabouts for a pile of rubble that marks the site of Arx Ruohim, modelled on the defensive castles of Henry VIII that you observed in and around Deal, and supposedly replacing a tower erected by King Vortigern.

Easy cliff walking now takes you past Foreness Point and Long Nose Spit, which is the most northerly point on the Isle of Thanet, and the most northerly location you have so far reached. From here all your walking as far as Faversham will be in a westerly or south-westerly direction, and you really will now feel you have turned the corner. The cliff scenery hereabouts is really splendid: look out at Botany Bay for a giant rock stack that brings to mind another feature of the Dorset coast, namely the Old Harry rock stacks near Swanage. Once past Long Nose Spit, you get your first views of the huge urban sprawl comprising Cliftonville and Margate. At the time of writing the Viking Coastal Trail was being diverted away from the cliff edge at Long Nose Spit, and it was impossible to stick to the cliff top, but the slight diversion away from the cliff edge is well signposted and hopefully the cliff path will have been effectively reinstated once you read this. Assuming all is well, the continuation of the coastal walk to Margate is straightforward, your clifftop route following alongside Prince's Walk, then Queen's Promenade, Newgate Promenade and Fort Promenade in quick succession. There are plenty of options, all providing good sea views: you could simply walk along the promenades, or walk beside them, or in fact proceed by the seashore along the extensive sands, passing Palm Bay and Walpole Bay. To your left, as you walk along Prince's Walk and Queen's Promenade, is Cliftonville, a suburb of Margate which is set well back from the sea and is not really worth a special detour inland, although it boasted a fine hotel in Queen's Gardens called the Queen's Highcliffe. Now you swing quite markedly south-westwards towards the centre of Margate, descending to the seafront and looking straight ahead to The Bay, protected on its north-east side by the harbour wall and pier, which you may feel is surprisingly modest for such a big resort; this rounded stone arm was built by Rennie between 1810 and 1815, while the porticoed customs house building at its landward end was built in 1812. Separating

The Captain Digby inn at Kingsgate provides welcome refreshment on the Broadstairs to Margate stage of the walk, superb views from its garden to Kingsgate Bay and nearby cliffs, and easy access to the extraordinary buildings of Lord Holland.

The Bay from the mainland is a huge expanse of sand which you can expect to be crowded with sunbathers in the summer. You join The Parade and go forward to Marine Drive, now on the seafront, then follow Marine Drive to its junction with Marine Terrace; on the landward side of Marine Terrace is the site of the now defunct Dreamland Family Fun Park, and to your left is Margate's principal shopping area, with all the amenities you would expect of a large popular seaside town. Turn right on to Marine Terrace, soon reaching a roundabout from which it is a short walk to the station on your left. This section ends at the roundabout.

Kent's answer to Durdle Door – the splendid rock arch in the steep cliffs on the north side of Kingsgate Bay which is one of the highlights of this section.

Margate

Despite being one of the Cinque Ports (though not one of the original five), Margate has not achieved lasting status as a seaport in the same way that its neighbour Ramsgate has. There was a sea battle off the town in 1387, during the Hundred Years War, in which the Earl of Arundel led the English to a victory over the French and her allies, but historically it has hardly been a place of real strategic significance; Margate's fame has rather been as a pioneer in the business of promoting the coast as a leisure destination. A local glovemaker and Quaker named Benjamin Beale invented the covered bathing machine in 1753 and this helped attract large crowds to the town, which in turn quickly developed as a resort with people keen to join in the new craze for sea bathing. By 1775 there were thirty bathing machines in use in the town: the machines were enclosed wagons, transporting swimmers from changing rooms to the sea, and once pushed out to sea, the bather would leave them and enjoy his swim. They were described in 1790 as "at once simple and convenient, and the pleasures and advantages of bathing may be enjoyed in so private a manner as to be consistent with the strictest delicacy." This new craze for bathing of course pre-dated the arrival of the railway, and so visitors would arrive from London by boat. For many years boat travellers were forced to use a clumsy craft known as the "Margate hoy," whose unpredictable movements led to many a case of sea-sickness, but around 1815 these craft were replaced by steamers. Spence refers to a picture of the steamer arriving at the old jetty in 1869, describing the scene as" a confusion of parasols, portmanteaux, shoeshine boys, reunited families and cheerful excursionists." Indeed during the 19th century the town became a magnet for Londoners in the summer, many of them working-class, and to this day it retains a reputation for being a somewhat down-market resort, arguably more so than any other in Kent. Certainly the seafront, dominated by one particularly tall, and particularly ugly, tower block, lacks any of the style and dignity of many other south-east resorts. The Dreamland theme park, opened early in the 20th century and boasting a Grade II listed roller-coaster ride, could be regarded as the epitome of at best unsophisticated, at worst tacky, entertainment, and few tears were shed, amongst students of architecture at any rate, when it finally closed in 2003. One thing Margate as a seaside resort lacks is a long pier; the old jetty, built in the 1800's, was badly damaged by fire in 1964, and most of it was destroyed by severe weather in 1978.

There are few buildings of real architectural merit in Margate, perhaps the best being the old parish church of St John, at the south end of the High Street. Built on the site of an old Saxon church, it has a very long nave, some late Norman arcading and a large collection of brasses dating back to the 15th century. Also of interest is the medieval Salmestone Grange in Nash Road well inland from the coast, one of the most important granges of St Augustine's Abbey, dating back to the early 14th century; the Greek-style early 19th century Royal Sea Bathing Hospital in Canterbury Road; the flint Drapers' Almshouses in St Peter's Road, founded in 1708; the brown- brick and red-brick India House in Hawley Street, dating back to 1767 and described by Pevsner as the best house in Margate; the clock tower erected in 1889 to commemorate Queen Victoria's Jubilee; and the Tudor half-timbered house on the corner of Trinity Hill and King Street, which became a museum. There are also some good examples of 18th and 19th century terraces in Cecil Square, Holy Trinity Square, Fort Hill and Fort Crescent. But the overwhelming impression architecturally is one of mediocrity; Spence writes that "Margate is lacking in any sense of style...You feel that nobody cares very much what happens to it as long as the bingo tellers are kept busy, the fruit machines and video games are milking the holidaymakers of their cash, and there is enough room between the parked coaches for the odd car to squeeze through." The town does, however, enjoy nine miles of sandy beach, and on Grotto Hill there is a subterranean folly known as the Grotto, believed to date from about 1800, with chambers carved out of the solid chalk, linked by subterranean passages, all covered with shells in floral and geometrical patterns. Today, the town has a number of manufacturing industries, including pharmaceuticals, generators, car components, sign machinery and inks. Margate has some famous associations: the artist Tracey Emin was brought up in Margate, with some of her work being based on the town, and T.S. Eliot completed parts of his famous work The Waste Land in a shelter overlooking the sands, while staying in neighbouring Cliftonville. Sitcom connoisseurs may recall that one of the funniest Only Fools And Horses Christmas specials, The Jolly Boys' Outing, was partly filmed in Margate, and the episode ended with Chas and Dave's Margate song which achieved no 46 in the charts in July 1982.

Kent's answer to Old Harry: the impressive rock stacks at Botany Bay just east of Margate.

Looking out to sea at Margate on a cloudless November day.

SECTION 6 - **MARGATE TO HERNE BAY**

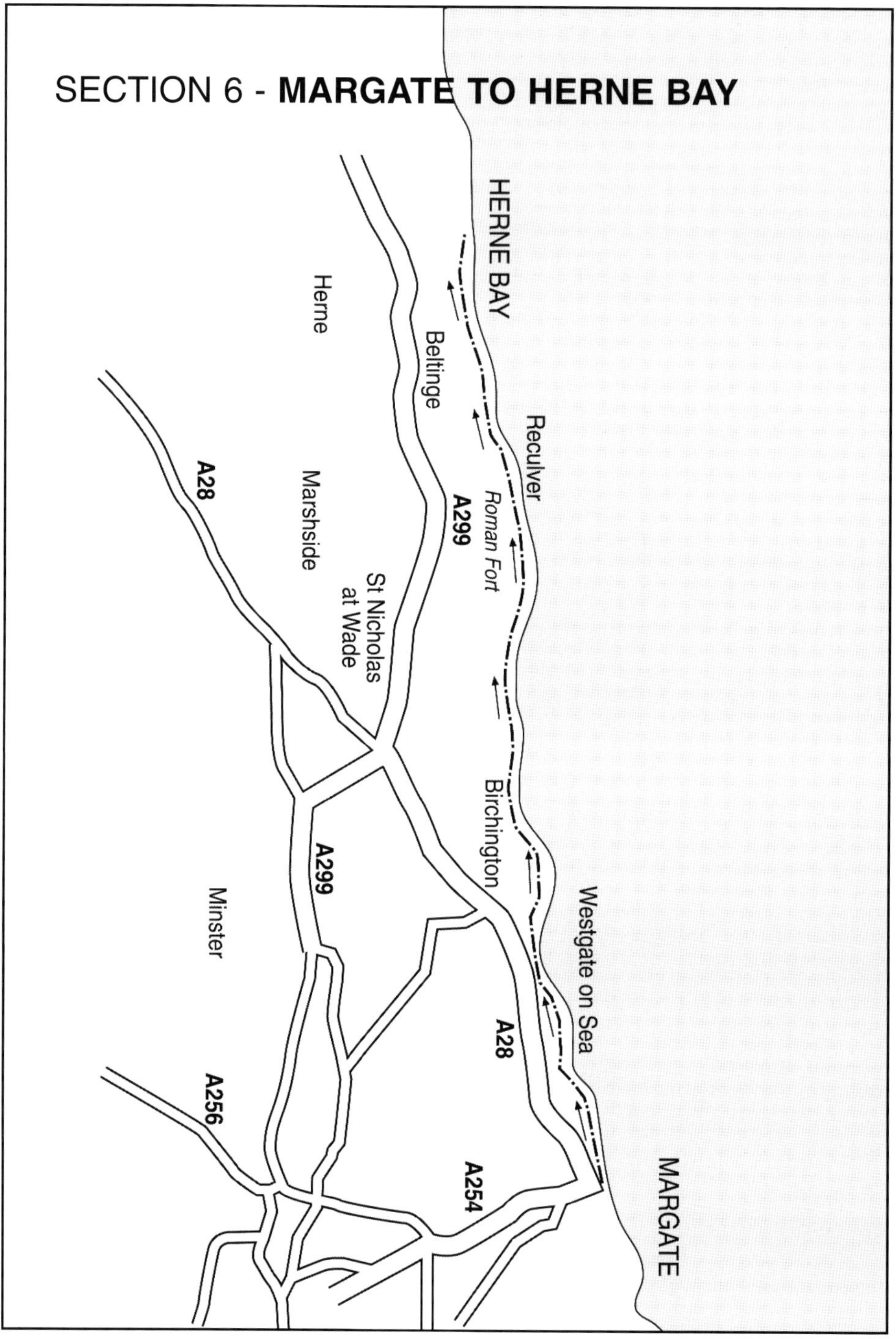

SECTION 6 - **MARGATE TO HERNE BAY**

Distance:	11 miles.
Route:	Margate - Westbrook Bay - Westgate-on-Sea - Birchington - Reculver - Herne Bay.
Map:	OS Explorer Sheet 150.
Public Transport:	Excellent train service between Margate and London Victoria via Birchington and Herne Bay (two trains an hour most days).
Conditions:	This section provides very straightforward and easy walking, and has a little bit of everything: some lovely cliff walking, constantly changing landscapes, fascinating rock formations, a monument of exceptional historical interest, and at the end, a cheerful seaside town with ample amenities and plenty of refreshment possibilities.
Refreshments:	See Appendix

Immediately beyond the roundabout by Margate railway station, you proceed along a wide concrete promenade and indeed will have this for company for all but a few hundred yards of the walk on to Minnis Bay beyond Birchington. To begin with, the view to your left, across a dreary suburban landscape, is frankly uninspiring, but the prospect to your right, with the beach, the rocks and the sea, is inviting indeed, and you could well be forgiven on hotter days for breaking off from your endeavours, pulling off your boots and enjoying a paddle in the water. Soon you come to Westbrook Bay with a rich variety of marine life to be found within its waters or on the shore, including starfish mussels, shoe crab, goby and dog whelk; among the birds you may see are the the sanderling and curlew, while plants to be found here include the bladder wrack, serrated wrack and oarweed. A rocky peninsula - indeed there are extensive rock formations from here all the way to Birchington - separates Westbrook Bay from St Mildred's Bay just to the west, then at the rocks of Ledge Point there is quite a pronounced swing to the south to reach Westgate-on-Sea. Westgate-on-Sea, which unsurprisingly looks out on to Westgate Bay, seems effectively like an extension of Margate, for there has been no real break in the suburban sprawl since the start of the section, but it is quieter and less garish than Margate, and boasts some most attractive gardens. It was developed as a seaside resort in the 1870's, and by the end of the 19th century the sea-front was lined two-deep with, to quote Pevsner, "big jolly houses, very typical of those years, of bright red brick, largely hung with orangey tiles and breaking out into plentiful gables, bow-windows, and balconies." It also acquired its own golf course, cricket club and lawn tennis club.

Leaving Westgate-on-Sea you approach Epple Bay, keeping to the promenade throughout. In due course, however, you arrive at a sign which warns you that the promenade will soon peter out, so at this point you need to climb the steps to Sea Road, turn right into this road and follow it briefly, keeping a golf course to your left. Soon, however, a path going off to your right allows access down to the resumption of the promenade, and it is then a quite extraordinary walk on to the front at Birchington, with steep chalk cliffs towering above you to your left and the rocky shore to your right, full of interest for the beachcomber, geologist and nature lover. It is safe, easy walking in spectacular surroundings. The height of the cliff faces to your left means that you are in a sense cut off from civilisation, and although the sprawl of Birchington is in reality just a short distance away, you somehow feel as though you are in quite remote and inhospitable country. This surely is one of the most underrated and fascinating parts of the north Kent coast, and it is a pity when the cliffs relent and the chalk dips below ground, signifying your arrival at Birchington. There are no amenities in Birchington that actually lie on the seafront, and you will need to go inland to reach them; there is a shop conveniently reached via Minnis Road off the Parade beyond the western end of the cliffs, but the station and principal shopping area of Birchington may be found about a mile inland via Minnis Road and Station Road.

Birchington

Birchington was developed as a seaside community in the late 1860's. The owner of the land on which development took place was the architect J.P. Seddon, who was responsible for building six Tower Bungalows in Spencer Road, of which four remain, in Indian idiom, with each house boasting a stocky tower at the landward end. Otherwise, Birchington's only buildings of real architectural interest are All Saints Church which dates back to Norman times and is noteworthy for its fine collection of monuments, and the early 19th century mansion at Quex Park, but both are well inland. The village was the home of the artist and poet Dante Gabriel Rossetti who lived here until his death in 1882 - he was buried in All Saints' churchyard - while bridge enthusiasts may be amused to note the fact that the village of Acol lies just south of Quex House Gardens.

Although it is a shame to leave the cliffs behind, you now enjoy a fine walk alongside Minnis Bay, noteworthy not only for beautiful sands but for its variety of bird life, with redshank, turnstone, oystercatcher, dunlin and godwit among many species to be found here. For a while your trusty concrete promenade continues alongside the bay, but when it ends you simply bear left to join an excellent concrete path, remaining close to the sea; although the path is narrower than the promenade you've followed almost all the way from Margate, it it is extremely well maintained and provides excellent fast

The walk from Margate to Birchington, with its cliffs and wide promenade for much of the way, is one of the most underrated sections of the Kent coast. This is the view back towards Margate from Birchington.

walking. Despite the fact that the cliffs have been left behind, the urban sprawl which has persisted along the north Kent coast really all the way from Kingsgate now relents and you can now enjoy fine views across miles of unspoilt countryside to your left. The tranquillity is only disturbed by the noise of trains from the railway that runs across the fields, but the modern trains are noticeably quieter than their predecessors and it may be comforting to coast walkers using the trains to know that they are actually running! Ahead of you, there is a very conspicuous tall building, towering above the surrounding flat fields and coastline: this is the most impressive ruin of the old church of St Mary at Reculver, one of the most prominent landmarks on the whole of the Kent coast. The going along the approach to Reculver is fast, easy and enjoyable, with a surface that is firm and clear, the sea just at hand to your right, extensive views inland, and the prospect of the old church ruin which gets more and more magnificent as you continue. Just under two miles from Birchington you are joined to your left by the River Wantsum, your meeting with this river signifying your official exit from the Isle of Thanet; you walk briefly parallel with it, then enjoy further easy walking along the coastal path to reach Reculver and the ruins of St Mary's Church.

Reculver

Reculver has a long history. It is believed that in 43 AD the Romans under Emperor Claudius set up a small initial camp here because of its safe harbour; it was the site of the Roman fort of Regulbium, which is believed to date back to the first half of the 3rd century, and evidence

The twin towers of Reculver, built in the 12th century and saved from removal with the rest of the church because of its usefulness as a navigational aid for sea vessels. It is now one of the best-loved landmarks on the north Kent coast.

suggests that it was earlier than most of the Roman shore forts. The fort stands on a hillock overlooking the sea - which incidentally has claimed a third of the original fortified area - and in its original state it was almost square, covering an area of over seven acres, with walls that were about 8 ft thick and 20 ft high. There was a Christian church here from the 7th century, in Saxon times; the church, built by King Ethelbert's successor Egbert, was the latest of the group built during this period by St Augustine and his converts. The Normans later added substantially to it, and from then it remained almost intact until as comparatively recently as the first decade of the 19th century. In that decade, to prevent it falling into the sea, much of the building was removed to St Mary's at Hillborough, leaving little more than the foundations, and the twin-towered western façade that was added in the 12th century; the purpose of leaving this part of the church was to enable it to act as a sea-mark on the cliff-top for ships in the Thames Estuary. It was off the coast near Reculver that much of the testing of Barnes Wallis' bouncing bomb was carried out prior to its deployment in the famous Dam Busters raids on German industrial targets in 1943, the twin towers of the church being chosen as the release point for the bombs as they resembled the towers at the Mohne and Eder dams in Germany, which were subsequently attacked. The man who tested the bomb was Wing Commander Guy Gibson, who following the raid was awarded the Victoria Cross. Today Reculver is a beautiful and peaceful place, a natural stopping place on your walk to Herne Bay, and there is a good range of amenities including a pub, café and visitor centre.

Having detoured to inspect the church ruin, go forward over the road and past the pub (the café is a little way beyond the pub down the road to the left), continue on to the car park and then walk through it, passing the visitor centre. You are now reunited with the Saxon Shore Way and, with the exception of an optional detour just west of Whitstable, and the walk round the Isle of Sheppey, you will stay with the Saxon

Shore Way right through to the other side of Rochester. Beyond the car park the going could not be clearer, as you strike out just south of west on a good path across the tops of the sandstone and clay cliffs which date back some 60 million years, getting good views ahead now to Herne Bay, the next big town on your journey. Having reached the highest point of the cliffs you go forward to a green area at the end of which a clear path, which you follow, leads away down the hillside. Soon you reach another path junction, the main path maintaining height and going on towards some trees, but you fork right on to a narrower path, shortly descending steps to find yourself on the beach, looking up to your left at a steep gully in the cliff face. There follows a very (and some might say mercifully) brief walk along the shingle, but in no time you scramble on to a grassy ledge that shortly becomes a proper wide concrete promenade, and now it is a good easy walk on to Herne Bay, with a grassy hillside to your immediate left; note a rather handsome thatched house much further up the hill as you go. A barrier prohibiting vehicular access signifies your arrival at the sailing club, but you continue round (or under) the barrier, and on past the fleet of sailing craft, soon finding yourself walking along the seafront at Herne Bay, with a huge number of eateries to choose from should you require refreshment. Continue through or round the car park to reach the pier where this section ends. To access the station, turn left up Station Road immediately before the pier; it is quite a long walk to the station, and will feel all the more so after a long day's walking, so be warned.

Herne Bay

The original village of Herne actually lies a mile and a half from the centre of modern Herne Bay. It was in the early 1830's that one Samuel Hacker of Canterbury spearheaded the development of what was merely a nearby fishing village into the popular seaside resort it is today, although a small planned development had been in existence since 1816-17. It once boasted the second longest pier in England, built in 1832, the construction stretching out to sea for a good three quarters of a mile; the reason for its length was to allow boats from London to be met more quickly, with stagecoaches waiting to transport passengers to Dover for ferries to the continent. In 1970 the pier pavilion was burnt down, being replaced in 1975-76, and in 1979 the pier was severed by storms, rendering the "offshore" section inaccessible. To compensate, so to speak, there was constructed a new long slim harbour wall known as Neptune's Arm, and holidaymakers and trippers can now stroll down Neptune's Arm and enjoy grandstand views across the bay. On a clear day it may also be possible to see the outlines of a cluster of metal forts built during World War 2, and intended to guard the Thames Estuary and deter German aircraft from flying up the Thames to bomb London, although they were constructed too late to be of any practical use. The pier was not the only victim of natural phemonena in Herne Bay in recent times: in February 1953, following a tidal surge which breached the sea defences, its promenade was buried under thousands of tons of shingle and roads were blocked by smashed boats.

Architecturally there is little of real interest in the town. Its focal point is its 80ft high clock

This is the lovely view enjoyed by the walker setting foot for Herne Bay from Reculver, which despite its small size boasts a pub, café, shop and visitor centre.

tower built by Edwin Dangerfield in 1837 using Portland stone and incorporating a mixture of Greek Doric and Corinthian columns. Standing roughly in the centre of the promenade, it is thought to be the first ever free standing purpose built clock tower, but Pevsner was unimpressed with it, describing the design as "inept" and the tower itself "hurriedly finished off." Among the more interesting conventional buildings of Herne Bay are those of Hanover Square, laid out as one of three squares of the new town; St George's Terrace, opposite the end of the pier, which in Spence's words, "makes some attempt at seafront dignity;" and what Pevsner describes as a "good patch" in Marine Terrace, built in 1830-35 on Central Parade. Like the clock tower, the stuccoed Pier Hotel, originally the Assembly Rooms, has Corinthian features, and if you wish to know more about the history and architecture of the area there is a museum in the tourist information centre near the clock tower. A perhaps less aesthetically pleasing building, although one you should try and see, is the new pier pavilion which, as stated above, was built in 1975-76, and is entertainingly described by Pevsner as a " zany affair, clad in corrugated aluminium, and crowned with a row of hexagonal clerestory lights of turquoise plastic." The town, stated by Spence to be a "quiet, old-fashioned resort which is now enjoying something of a revival," certainly seems less brash and garish than Margate, and perhaps therefore a pleasanter place for the coastal walker to linger. On a humorous note, in recent years it has become particularly popular with elderly folk, which explains its rather unkind nickname, Hernia Bay.

Two views of from the lovely cliff path between Reculver and Herne Bay. Right: looking back towards the twin towers of Reculver. Below: looking ahead to the pleasant and popular resort of Herne Bay.

SECTION 7 - **HERNE BAY TO FAVERSHAM**

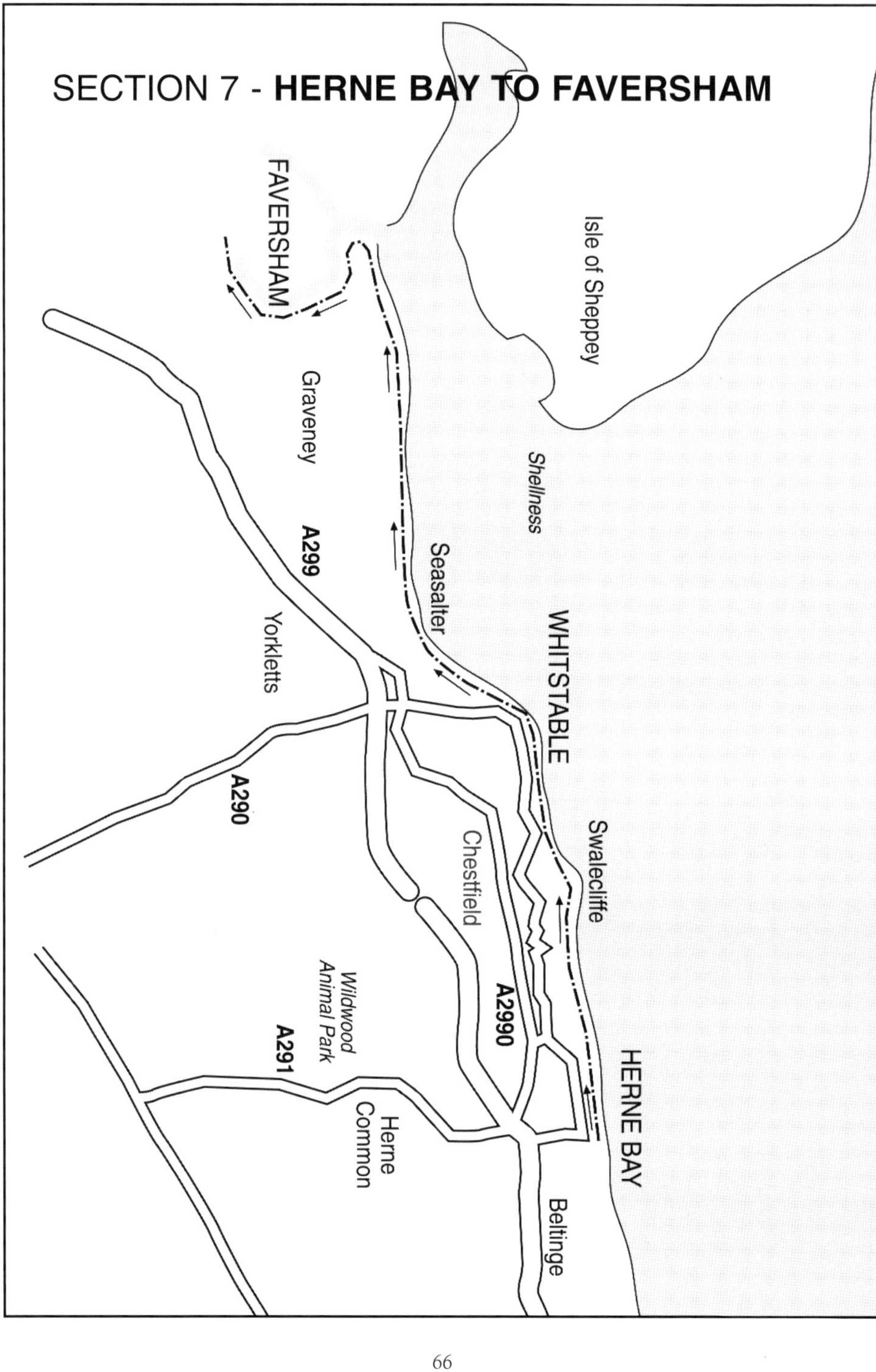

SECTION 7 - **HERNE BAY TO FAVERSHAM**

Distance:	11 miles.
Route:	Herne Bay - Swalecliffe - Tankerton - Whitstable - Seasalter - Swale Estuary - Faversham Creek - Faversham.
Map:	OS Explorer Sheets 150 and 149.
Public Transport:	Excellent train service linking Herne Bay, Swalecliffe, Whitstable and Faversham with London Victoria and Margate (two trains an hour most days).
Conditions:	This is good easy walking for the most part, with metalled promenades or clear footpaths, and just one slightly awkward section between Whitstable and Seasalter.
Refreshments:	See Appendix.

Beyond the pier you continue to follow the promenade, going forward to a metalled walkway along the back of the beach with only beach huts obscuring your view of the coast; this walkway is extremely popular and you are unlikely to be on your own especially at weekends. There is a brief let-up in the concrete as you pass by the nondescript settlement of Swalecliffe, the path becoming a stony track through an area of grass, but the concrete soon returns as you come to Tankerton, now effectively an appendage of Whitstable and certainly not worth leaving the coast path to visit. It did once boast a pier, which was opened in 1893 but was demolished in 1913. This is a walk of contrasts: to your left is a vast array of aesthetically unpleasing holiday homes, while a signboard beside the path tells you to look out for a rare moth known as agnopoterix putridella and a rare plant called hogs fennel! Still making excellent progress, you pass the impressive Continental Hotel, the sturdiest structure you will have gone by since leaving Herne Bay, and head for the very prominent works lying straight ahead of you, situated at the east side of the Whitstable harbour area. Just before the works you arrive at a T-junction, where your confident coastal progress is halted in its tracks; you are forced to turn left here, and proceed towards the road that is clearly visible ahead. Shortly before the road, however, look out for a sign for the Indoor Bowling Centre, and immediately opposite this sign turn right, aiming to the right of the Harbour Office, to proceed through a bustling pedestrian precinct including a fish market. Turn right by the RNLI building then shortly left, behind the boats, to find yourself on another concrete walkway; this is as close as you will get to the centre of Whitstable, and you may well wish to leave the coast here to explore the old town.

Whitstable

The somewhat unusual name for this town is thought to derive either from "hwit stapol" (white post), possibly referring to a post marking a suitable landing place for shipping, or "witan stapol" (councillor's post), referring to a post marking a meeting place. The town stands at the mouth of the Swale estuary, about 8 miles north of Canterbury, and was a stopping place for pilgrims heading for the cathedral city. In earlier centuries Whitstable was the port for Canterbury, although none of the medieval town remains save for All Saints Church which has in any case been extensively rebuilt. The first passenger-carrying steam railway in the world was opened between Whitstable and Canterbury in 1830; it was known as the Crab and Winkle line and continued until 1953. The writer W Somerset Maugham lived in Whitstable as a child, and the actor Peter Cushing lived in the town between 1959 and his death in 1994.

Described as a "modest, low-key seaside resort," the name Whitstable is almost synonymous with oysters, which have long been cultivated here; there is an oyster and fishery exhibition by the harbour side, and there is still an Oyster Feast held here each September. In former times the so-called Whitstable Natives grew wild on the seabed, but nowadays farmed Pacific oysters are bred in tanks and mature on oyster beds in the shallows. Tradition has it that you may only eat natives when there is an R in the month but you can eat Pacific oysters when there is a D in the day - in other words, at any time! Whitstable is also well known as a

The harbour at Whitstable on a cloudless mid-summer evening. The prominent building to the right is a popular restaurant where locals and holidaymakers can tuck into the local delicacy, Pacific oysters.

Looking across the sands at Whitstable to the Old Neptune pub. Its seaside setting means that it is a magnet for visitors especially in summer.

yachting as well as fishing centre; between the High Street and the sea are the Walls, including Island Wall and Middle Wall, with its rows of fishermen's cottages of black and white weatherboarding. The weatherboarded and tarred Beach Stores, on the beach, are reputed to have been for hanging nets and sails out to dry, but although comparison with the so called "net houses" on the beach at Hastings immediately springs to mind, the ones at Whitstable are quite different. To quote Spence, "Whitstable's streets are filled with the metallic slap of rigging twanged by the wind, from small boats beached in alleys or backyards, and out on the mudflats bent figures delve about for bait or shellfish." Architecturally there is little or nothing to see in Whitstable: the principal church, All Saints in Church Street, was largely rebuilt in around 1875, while on Tower Hill is a small castellated mansion called the Castle, the earliest part of which consists of an octagonal tower of flint and red brick, dating back to around 1827. The Sir William Nottidge School in Belle Vue Road, dating back to 1952, is described by Pevsner as a "large, excellently detailed group, crisp and refined" but it is hardly worth making a special detour for. The town does claim to have the oldest golf clubhouse in England!
As you leave Whitstable behind, the going is initially easy and straightforward, and you can enjoy the remarkable variety in the backs of the buildings to your left. You pass to the inland side of the Old Neptune pub, a very popular watering hole especially in summer, then continue along the path, looking out to sea. Just beyond a row of houses where some colourful mosaics have been incorporated into the walls, look out for a Saxon Shore Way signposted pointing left, along a path heading inland. You need to take this path which proceeds to a T-junction with Island Wall. Turn right onto this road and follow it, then when Island Wall bends decisively to the right, carry straight

on, following the Saxon Shore Way signpost along a clear track. The track then bends left to cross a golf course, aiming for a footbridge over the railway. Cross the railway by the footbridge then bear immediately right along a path that runs parallel with the railway, enjoying good views out to sea. Follow the path to its end at a T-junction of paths at which you turn left, then walk uphill to arrive at Joy Lane; turn right and follow this lane downhill, passing a pub and soon reaching a road going off to the right (Florence Road is more or less opposite it to the left). Turn right onto this road and cross the railway, then turn immediately left into Admiralty Walk, following it and going forward to Fairway Crescent and Preston Parade. As you continue down Preston Parade you become aware of a path closer to the shore on your right, but this is not in fact a public path. Follow Preston Parade to its end, now back at the shore level again with a shingle beach in front of you. This is a private beach area, so you need to take the path along the back of the beach which brings you to the main road at the village of Seasalter, close to the Blue Anchor. Turn right onto the road, marked on maps here as Faversham Road, and now follow it westwards, separated from the shore by housing. Just beyond Minstrell Farm, the housing to your right relents and a good path establishes itself along the back of the shore, then a short way ahead you arrive at the convenient Seasalter store and café which provides a very welcome on-route refreshment opportunity. Beyond the store, you keep the road to your left for a while, but after half a mile or so the road swings away to the left while your path, having initially swung left with the road, bears right by a roadside pub - presenting another good refreshment opportunity! - to proceed parallel with the shore once more. During the Napoleonic Wars, the pub, Ye Old Sportsman, was a meeting point for local smugglers with French prisoners of war who were helped by the smugglers to escape back to France. Superb walking now ensues on an excellent green path,with the sea close by to your right, and Nagden Marshes to your left; this is a key point on your walk, for on your right you will now be looking out not to open sea, but across the mouth of the Swale estuary to the south shoreline of the Isle of Sheppey. Unless you choose to follow the optional Sheppey detour, you will not see the open sea again until you reach the north shore of the Isle of Grain at the mouth of the Thames Estuary. Continue westwards on an excellent path, now walking through the South Swale Nature Reserve which boasts a large variety of species of bird including the reed warbler, lapwing, redshank, skylark, dunlin, meadow pipit, bearded tit, marsh harrier and rare little tern, while plant life includes yellow-horned poppy, sea kale, sea beet, vipers bugloss, dragons' teeth, biting stonecrop and golden samphire. The views are extensive and impressive in all directions.

Progress is for a while excellent, but you soon reach a significant natural obstruction, namely the mouth of Faversham Creek, and you now find yourself forced significantly inland for the first time since you returned to Pegwell Bay from Richborough. Your path swings to the left, away from the sea along the banks of the creek heading for the town of Faversham; the creek twists and meanders quite considerably, and for a while the path is actually taking you in an easterly direction, seemingly further away from your destination. However, the path is well defined, the surroundings are unspoilt and attractive, and after passing the buildings of Nagden the path swings resolutely towards Faversham, with good views towards the town and especially its prominent church steeple about which more below. As the buildings of Faversham get closer, there becomes a slightly suburban feel to the surroundings; ignoring paths going away to the left, you stick to the creekside path and in due course you pass through a boatyard, signalling your entry to Faversham, one of the most beautiful towns on your journey. Follow the footpath signs carefully, soon arriving at a T-junction with a road, where you must now leave the creekside, bearing left to pass the welcome Anchor pub and then immediately right into Abbey Street. This is a delightful street which in architectural terms comes as a very welcome relief after the somewhat bland buildings of Seasalter. Go forward to arrive at the Market Place in the town centre, where this section ends.

Faversham

The name Faversham, derived from "foeferes-ham" meaning "smith's homestead or village," is one of the most important and also attractive towns you will meet on your walk along the Kent coast. Faversham Creek, which you will have enjoyed ever since leaving the shoreline, was in use as early as Roman times, and the Romans had a settlement in the vicinity named Durolevum; by the 12th century the place had risen to prominence as a manufacturing centre and a port, and in due course became a member of the Confederation of Cinque Ports. There are reminders of Faversham's importance as a port in Conduit Street, behind the Shepherd Neame brewery, where you can see a 15th century timbered town storehouse, and also at Iron Wharf, not far from the end of Abbey Street, where a number of preserved sailing barges are berthed. Ever since the 12th

Probably the finest house in the finest street in Faversham: the timber-framed home of Thomas Arden, sometime town mayor, in Abbey Street.

century Faversham has been a busy commercial, agricultural and manufacturing centre. Agricultural produce includes cherries, apples and hops, and there are fruit canning, grading and packing stations; the town still has a brickmaking industry; it is home to the famous Shepherd Neame brewery which has been brewing beer since 1698 and calls itself the country's oldest brewer; and at one time the town was particularly famous for its explosives industry, the Chart Gunpowder Mills opening in 1760 and the town continuing to produce explosives until the 1930's. The Chart Gunpowder Mills, off South Road have now been restored, and it is possible to view the manufacturing process used for the explosives.

As well as being a bustling commercial centre, Faversham remains one of England's best preserved historic towns, the prosperity of former times being reflected in its array of Tudor, Stuart and Georgian buildings. Arguably the finest street in the town is Abbey Street, which has been restored as a complete period piece. In this street is the former home of Thomas Arden, who was a mayor of the town and one of the town's leading citizens until he was murdered in his home by his wife's lover in 1551. The timber-framed house in which Arden lived incorporates the only remains of the town's medieval abbey; the abbey itself, originally a Cluniac and subsequently a Benedictine abbey, was erected by Stephen, King of England in the 12th century, and was excavated in 1965, while the former Fleur de Lis Inn, where Arden's murder was plotted, has survived and served in recent years as a Heritage centre which opened in 1977. It has excellent displays depicting Faversham's history and development down the centuries, with exhibits which include an old barber shop and model sailing barge. The continuation of Abbey Street is Court Street, described by Spence as "wide and dignified, a good mixture of timbered gables and overhangs, Georgian brickwork and Victorian frontages, all harmonising together."

Perhaps the area of the town richest in fine buildings is Market Place, which is dominated by the Guildhall with its combination of rough 16th century timber arcade, complete with robust wooden pillars, and a Regency superstructure. The nearby New Royal cinema, incidentally, boasts the largest screen in Kent! No. 10 in the Market Place is an overhanging black and white timber-framed building which dates back to 1570, while No. 12 was once an inn where King James II was held by local fishermen when trying to flee the country. One other excellent town house of note is 121 West Street which dates back to 1697 and boasts three superb panels of ornamental plasterwork. The best ecclesiastical building is the Norman parish church of St Mary of Charity, a Gothic building with a Georgian nave together with arcades of Tuscan columns, built after the original nave was declared unsafe; other features of interest in the church include early 14th century paintings of New Testament scenes to be found on an octagonal pillar in the north transept, beautifully carved choir misericords including a flute player and demonic figures, and a Decorated stone tomb canopy which may be the burial place of King Stephen. Arguably the most remarkable feature of the church is the tall west tower, topped by a fretted stone pinnacle. The steeple, inspired by the steeple on one of Wren's London churches, was erected at the end of the 18th century, and it presents as an inspiring sight to travellers approaching the town. Next to the church is the old grammar school dated 1587, which subsequently became the Masonic Hall. The former village of Ospringe, now inside the town, has the Maison Dieu which dates back to the 13th century; it served as a hostel for Canterbury pilgrims, as well as having almshouses and a hospital, but was principally intended as a royal stopover on the road between Dover and London. It is now a museum.

A quiet corner in Faversham, one of the lesser Cinque Ports and a beautiful old town. This is an area of the Market Place and to the left of the picture is the Guildhall with its 16th century timber arcade and Regency superstructure.

SECTION 8 - **FAVERSHAM TO SWALE STATION**

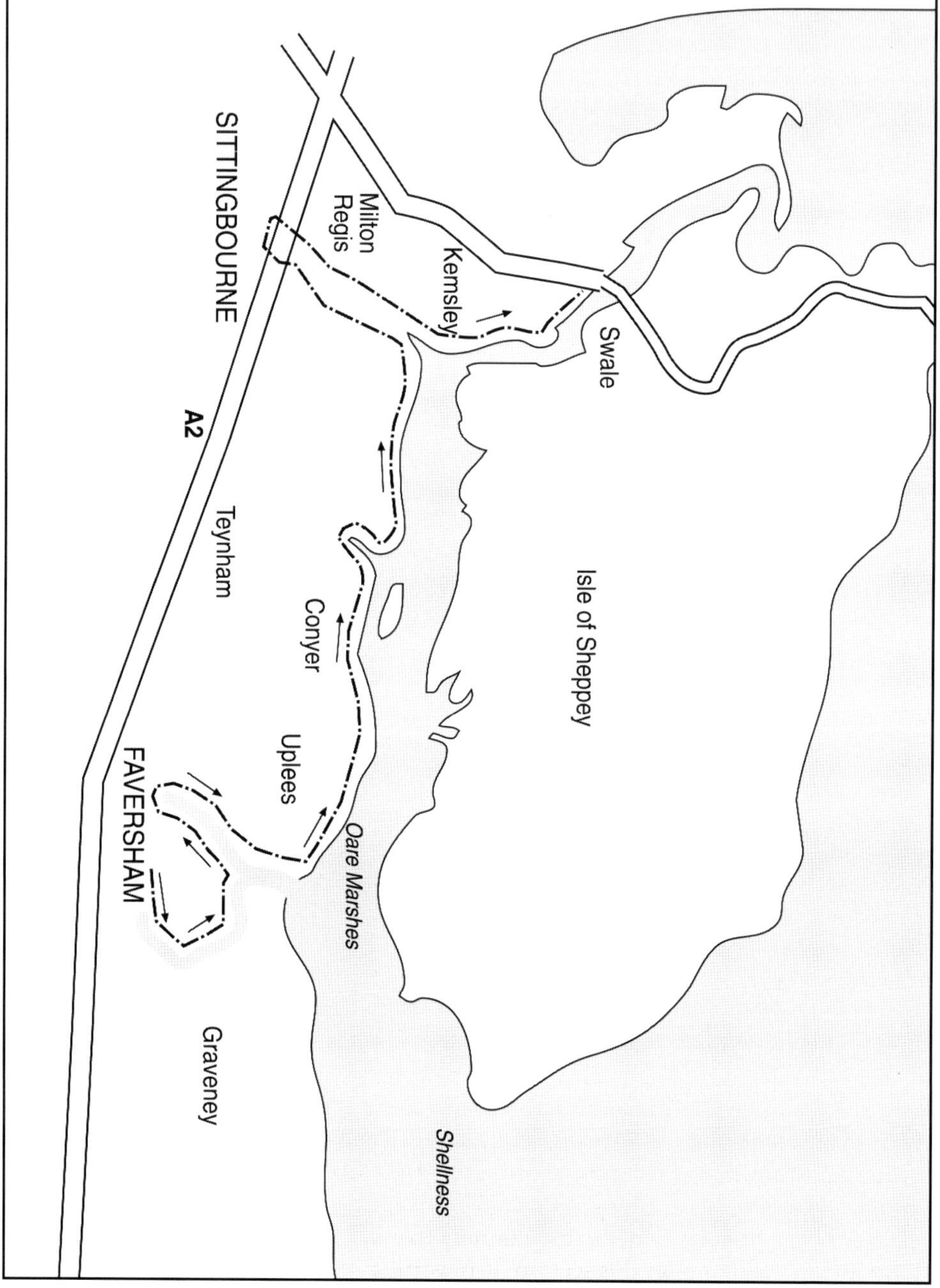

SECTION 8 - **FAVERSHAM TO SWALE STATION**

Distance:	17 miles(longer route); 14 miles(shorter route).
Route:	Faversham - Oare - Conyer - Sittingbourne - Kemsley Marshes - Swale Station.
Map:	OS Explorer Sheet 149.
Public Transport:	Excellent train services (two fast, two slow, trains each hour most days) linking Faversham and Sittingbourne with Rochester and London Victoria; slow trains also serve Teynham between Faversham and Sittingbourne. Regular trains (two an hour most days) linking Swale with Sittingbourne on the Sheerness branch line.
Conditions:	This is a tremendously varied and mostly very interesting walk on excellent paths, utilising the Saxon Shore Way for much of its length. The latter part of the walk could be somewhat depressing in grey or wet weather. Even if the shorter route is taken, this is a long walk, most of it into the prevailing wind, and you may prefer to split or shorten it by using the railheads at Teynham or Sittingbourne.
Refreshments:	See Appendix.

Assuming you detoured into the centre of Faversham, begin this section by retracing your steps from the market square to walk back along Court Street, then turn left into Partridge Lane and follow it down to North Lane. Turn right to walk along North Lane, then very shortly turn left to cross the bridge over Faversham Creek. At this point it seems an absurdly narrow stretch of water to have had to detour so far from the coast to negotiate!

Immediately beyond the bridge you have a choice. By far the *shorter* route, although certainly less picturesque, is as follows. Having crossed the bridge, turn immediately left into Brent Road, which follows parallel with the creek; the road then bends right, becoming Brent Hill and rising to reach a T-junction, entering the district of Faversham known as Davington. On the other side of the road at the T-junction is the 12th century Davington Priory Church with an adjacent house that incorporates the cloister of the original Benedictine nunnery that was founded in 1153. Although you have a long way to go on this section, it is worth a quick detour to visit. Turn right at

A reminder of Faversham's importance as a port in previous centuries: Oyster Bay House, dominating the banks of Faversham Creek.

the T-junction to follow Priory Row northwards, passing Davington Primary School which is situated to the left, then ignoring the Ham Road fork to the right, proceed along Oare Road. There is a large lake and then a sprawling industrial complex to the left, and an old windmill (a brick tower-mill without sails) to the right; just east of the mill are disused gravel pits on the site of one of Faversham's gunpowder works. Shortly, just short of the unremarkable village of Oare, you reach the junction with the B2045 signposted Sittingbourne M2, and arrive at Oare Creek.*

The *longer* route from the Faversham Creek crossing, which provides some superb creekside walking that you will otherwise miss, is as follows. Having crossed the bridge, turn immediately right, following the Saxon Shore Way signposts, keeping the creek to your right. Shortly you are forced away from the creekside to get round the left edge of the Brents Industrial Estate, but are then signposted right to return to the creek and an excellent embankment path. A lovely walk now follows alongside the creek, and you can look across to the path you used to reach Faversham from the coast a couple of miles back. The embankment path shortly becomes separated from the creek by an area of marshland, then swings north-westwards - watch for the impressive houses over the creek that you will remember passing on the previous section - and arrives at the undoubted highlight of the longer route, the white weatherboarded Shipwright's Arms which stands at the confluence of Faversham Creek and Oare Creek. There is an astonishingly remote feel to this pub, even though it is only a couple of miles from Faversham's bustling centre. Now swinging south-west, the clearly marked path proceeds along the east side of Oare Creek with its massive array of boats. The path becomes narrow and slightly rougher, but then widens into a proper metalled road which continues beside Oare Creek to the junction with Oare Road (at this point, marked on maps as The Street). Here, just short of the village of Oare and at the point asterisked at the end of the above paragraph, you are reunited with the shorter route. Proceed briefly along the road round the edge of the creek towards the pub on its western side, but before you reach the pub you turn right to follow the Saxon Shore Way, using a path that proceeds along the left bank of Oare Creek; this is excellent walking on a fine path which is initially muddy but becomes firmer as you progress back towards the coast. Look out for the church of St Peter on the escarpment to your left. Soon you reach the gateway to Oare Marshes with its huge array of wildlife and plant life: birds to look out for include the lapwing, snipe, redshank, shoveler, black-tailed godwit, whimbrel, curlew, wigeon, teal, gadwall, reed warbler and sedge warbler, among the insects are dragonflies and damselflies, and plants include reedmace, samphire, sea lavender and frogbit. Continue forward along the obvious path to arrive back at the coast, now looking out across the Swale, an estuarine strip of water which extends from above Whitstable to the east as far as the mouth of the Medway just west of Queenborough. Although on maps it looks like a river it is in fact a submerged valley which in Roman times was probably twice its present width. Nowadays the Swale does not see a huge number of vessels, but it was for centuries used by ships to gain access to London from the English Channel.

The white weatherboarded Shipwrights Arms, a beautiful and popular pub on the banks of Faversham Creek, with an excellent reputation for both its beer and its food.

There are fantastic views from this spot: you can admire the views back to the Shipwright's Arms and the confluence of Faversham and Oare Creeks, you may gaze eastwards out to the open sea with Seasalter and Whitstable clearly visible on a good day, and you can look across to Harty on the Isle of Sheppey, and its beautiful Norman church of St Thomas. Meanwhile, to the west you can see the massive new bridge crossing from the mainland to Sheppey which marks the end of this section, but don't be fooled, for although it looks near, it is actually still a very long way off. For now, the walking is straightforward and extremely enjoyable; continuing along the Saxon Shore Way, you swing westwards and follow a wide clear path proceeding beside the Swale. You pass the visitor centre at Harty Ferry, this name recalling the old and now defunct ferry crossing from here to Harty on the Isle of Sheppey, but this section, with the Swale to your right and acres of freshwater grazing marsh to your left, is otherwise quite remote and unspoilt. I walked it on a freezing cold November day into the teeth of a biting north-westerly wind but on a calm warm day this will be one of the loveliest most relaxing sections of the whole journey. The going remains easy for the next three miles or so. There are no obvious landmarks or unusual features to enable you to monitor your progress, save perhaps for a marshy island a little way out from the shore called Fowley Island which is a feeding ground for black-headed gulls and oystercatchers. The views to the Isle of Sheppey are absorbing, and will hopefully whet your appetite for your journey round the island which is described fully in sections 9 and 10.

Soon after getting level with Fowley Island the path swings inland to negotiate Conyer Creek. This creek was once full of barges transporting bricks from the works close to the village, and also fruit from the orchards nearby; there are many orchards in this area, helping to maintain Kent's reputation as the Garden

Nowadays Faversham Creek is more popular with the sailing fraternity than as a means of conveying goods by barge. This peaceful scene is only a half-hour walk from the bustling centre of Faversham.

of England. Incidentally Teynham, a short distance inland from here, is regarded as the birthplace of Kent's orchards, for it was the first place in Kent where apples and cherries were systematically grown, during the reign of Henry VIII in the 16th century. In Roman times vineyards flourished on the nearby slopes. Shortly you enter a small wooded area which comes as quite a surprising and welcome contrast to the very open exposed countryside of the past three miles. You emerge from the woodland to arrive at a T-junction with a lane, turning left to proceed into the village of Conyer. Pass the very tempting pub, then continue on to the south-eastern end of the harbour to reach the bottom end of Conyer Creek at another T-junction by a phone box. It is possible to access the station at Teynham, on the London Victoria-Sittingbourne-Faversham railway line, by turning left at the T-junction and following the road for a mile and a half. The coast route, however, turns right at the T-junction then immediately hard right again at a multi-footpath junction, following the Saxon Shore Way as signposted up the west side of the creek to return to the shoreline. If the signposting confuses you, simply aim for the path running closest to the creek and you will not go wrong! The walk back to the shoreline is somewhat more open and circuitous than the initial walk from the shoreline into the village, the path heading initially westwards then swinging eastwards to negotiate the south-west arm of the creek, then veering north-westwards before swinging just east of north to return to the main shoreline. It is then back to "business as usual," as you continue due westwards on a clear path beside the Swale, enjoying views to Sheppey to the right, and a varied but mainly rural north Kent landscape to your left. Although you are now nearing Sittingbourne there is no obvious sign of it just yet. Another old (and long disused) ferry crossing to Sheppey, the Elmley Ferry, was positioned along this stretch.

As you plough on, the huge Kemsley paper mill now becomes a dominant feature of the landscape ahead of you. The mill, though tantalisingly separated from you by Milton Creek, appears to be little more than a stone's throw away, but rather like Pegwell Bay many miles back, it takes a good deal longer to approach it than one somehow thinks it should. A major feature of the landscape to your left is Little Murston Nature Reserve with its large lake, the north part of which is marked on some maps as a disused oyster pond and is now a home to wildfowl. You reach the mouth of Milton Creek and you are now faced with a walk of two miles inland - all the way into Sittingbourne, in fact - to get round it, there being no available bridge crossing any nearer the main shoreline. Unfortunately, the majority of the walk from here to Sittingbourne is particularly depressing. It starts reasonably enough, with the nature reserve still visible to the left, and the paper mill, which is not without a certain dignity, most conspicuous across the creek. However after passing under the pylon lines your view to the nature reserve is blocked off by a rather ugly industrial works which are to your left, and a little beyond these works, the path leaves the creek, swings to the left into a huge industrial estate, and peters out. Where it does so, simply aim for the main road, named Castle Road and running north to south, using a crude path across a rough grassy area to reach this road. Now follow it southwards resolutely towards Sittingbourne, ignoring side turnings; unless you have an interest in 20th century suburban industrial architecture this walk is unfortunately extremely tedious. Keep trudging along, until you come to a road leading off to the right named Eurolink Way, just short of a dead end for traffic. Follow Eurolink Way westwards; it is theoretically possible just to keep along it to its end (asterisked below), bypassing the town centre of Sittingbourne completely. However in order to relieve the tedium of this part of the journey, and to enable you to take advantage of the amenities Sittingbourne has to offer, the approved route soon turns left off Eurolink Way following the cycle route signposted for the town centre. The cycle route passes under the railway then across the busy A2 and straight on down West Lane. At the next big junction turn right, and proceed westwards, soon finding yourself walking along Sittingbourne's main street. Although it is far from being the most attractive or charismatic town on your route, there are ample shops and eateries to enable you to recharge your batteries.

Sittingbourne

Sittingbourne is the most easterly of Kent's industrial towns, and you will already have noted the profusion of industrial development on your approach to the town centre. For centuries trade in brick, corn, fish and fruit flourished from the quays on Milton Creek, with Crown Quay serving as base for a fleet of spirit-sail barges; industries in the town today include the manufacture of paper (as you will have seen!), cement, bricks and clothing, as well as fruit packing and preserving. However it is not devoid of architectural merit, with a High Street which as Spence says, "still has the vestiges of a Georgian thoroughfare about it." There are a number of houses of 18th century origin, most notably the George Hotel and Martins Bank. Its finest building is arguably its big flint-built parish church of St Michael, much of which dates from the 13th and 14th centuries, while the large west tower was completed in the 15th century. The town has two quite unusual features. The first is an Avenue of Remembrance south of the High Street, lined on both sides with hornbeams, each bearing a plaque commemorating a local man killed in the First World War. The second is probably the town's biggest tourist attraction, the Sittingbourne & Kemsley Light Railway. This is the preserved southern half of the former Edward Lloyd Paper Mill/Bowater's Industrial Railway, a narrow-gauge steam railway which until 1969 was used to convey both raw materials and finished paper products between the mills at Sittingbourne and Kemsley, and the docks at Ridham on the banks of the Swale estuary. The railway was a 24-hour a day operation and an integral part of the production process. Today it is possible to travel behind the original locomotives on the preserved section of line, some of which have journeyed along these tracks for 100 years. The railway opens from Easter to September and facilities include a café, museum, souvenir shop, model railways and wildlife gardens. For further information contact 0871 222 1569 or 01622 755313. If you have time, you might also want to visit Milton Regis, a suburb of the town but much older, and boasting a superbly preserved 15th century court hall as well as a steep High Street with timber-framed and Georgian houses. Castle Rough, on Kemsley Down just to the north-east of the town and not far from Kemsley paper mill which you will pass shortly beyond Sittingbourne, is reputed to have been a Danish settlement in 893 AD following one of their raids.

Sittingbourne is hardly a mecca for the architectural historian but this is one real gem in the town centre: the 15th century flint-built west tower of the parish church of St Michael.

To continue to make progress along the coast, follow the town's main thoroughfare to Station Street, just beyond the new shopping complex on the right. Turn right along Station Street and make for the station straight ahead, using the pedestrian crossing to negotiate the maze of roads separating you from it. Beyond the crossing turn left and walk immediately past the front of the station buildings (there is an excellent train service from here to London or back to Faversham, if you feel you've done enough for today!) then go directly forward downhill beside Milton Road under the bridge adjoining the station, soon reaching a roundabout and junction with the western end of Eurolink Way*. Leave the roundabout by the main road (Mill Way) exit, and follow the road under the bridge to another roundabout. Go straight on over the roundabout, very shortly turning right into Gas Road (look for the Saxon Shore Way signpost here), passing underneath the Sittingbourne & Kemsley Light Railway alluded to above. Follow Gas Road towards what appears to be a dead end, with some works straight ahead, but just before the works watch for a Saxon Shore Way signpost directing you along a path heading off Gas Road to the right; you will in fact be following the Saxon Shore Way for the whole of the rest of this section. Following the signed Saxon Shore Way path, very soon you reach Milton Creek and you begin your long walk back to the coast. This is a much more rewarding ramble than the walk southwards into Sittingbourne, for the creek is immediately beside you to your right, and your journey may be enlivened by the sound of racing go-karts from the stadium just over the creek. Keep going along a clear well-defined path, and soon you will find yourself passing the paper mill; two firms operate here, dealing chiefly with recycled paper, but in fact paper has been made at Kemsley for the past two centuries. Your passing the mill signifies that you are almost back at the coast. Follow the clear path, with strict signs cautioning you to keep to it (the technically inaccurate wording SAXON WAY is used on a lot of the signs), towards the mouth of Milton Creek. The last part of the creekside walk sees your path swing east, and when you reach the mouth of the creek and rejoin the bank of the Swale you find you are veering north, with the Swale to your right and the Isle of Sheppey now a tantalisingly short distance across the estuary.

Now proceed once more beside the Swale, heading northwards; to your left are expanses of low-lying marshes and grassland, dotted with lakes and ditches, and with large and somewhat unsightly industrial developments built liberally upon them. It presents a less than pleasing contrast to the walking beside the open sea that you enjoyed on the previous section. The area of the Swale separating you from Sheppey at this point is known as Elmley Reach, and peering from the waters is a group of little islands that are picturesquely named The Lilies. Keep ploughing on, along a clear and well-defined path, past a remarkable jetty, then a little under half a mile beyond the jetty your path, having continued in a predominantly north-westerly direction since

The brand new bridge across the Swale linking the Isle of Sheppey with the mainland, opened in July 2006.

reaching the mouth of Milton Creek, swings decisively to the right. There is a Saxon Shore waymark to ensure you don't stray here. A few hundred yards beyond this right swing, keeping to a clear embankment path, you approach the massive Ridham Dock works and its boundary fence; just before the boundary fence a path goes off to the left, and you need to turn left on to this path and follow it. Don't get sucked along the wide track that goes away here to the left, but follow the narrower bank path that proceeds closely parallel with the boundary fence. At the south-west corner of the works, turn hard right to join a road that now proceeds parallel with the western boundary of the works; when this road swings right to follow the north boundary, go forward a little and then right along a rough embankment path which heads back towards the Swale. You cross over an industrial railway, built to link the main Sittingbourne-Sheerness line with Ridham Dock, then carry on along the path which proceeds just east of north to arrive back at the Swale. You swing left and having now successfully negotiated the Ridham works, proceed on beside the estuary.

As you walk, you are now nearing the Kings Ferry Bridge linking Sheppey with the mainland, and you have directly in front of you the brand new road crossing of the Swale which you have had in your sights almost all the way from the mouth of Faversham Creek. Prior to the building of a bridge here, there was a cable ferry across the Swale, and although at most times during the day crossing was free, the ferryman was entitled to free oyster fishing. A road and rail bridge was first built in 1861 and replaced in 1904 and again in 1960, and the new road bridge crossing was opened in July 2006. The Saxon Shore Way, which you continue to follow, carries on along a path beside the Swale, but this path peters out as a road, linking Ridham Dock with the former main Sittingbourne-Sheerness road and bridge crossing, comes in from the left. When you reach the end of the path, simply bear left and join the road by means of the gateway; turn right on to the road, using a short tunnel* to pass underneath the railway and adjacent road. This section ends here. To access Swale railway station, look out for a flight of stone steps to your left immediately upon emerging from the tunnel; at the top of the steps you then need to cross over a barrier, walk to the right for a few yards then cross the road with care to arrive at the slipway leading up to the station. There are very regular rail services to Sittingbourne from here, just 9 minutes away by train, but the station has no facilities - not even a shelter - so if it is dark, cold or wet, keep your fingers crossed that the trains are running properly!

SECTION 9 - **SWALE STATION TO LEYSDOWN-ON-SEA VIA HARTY**

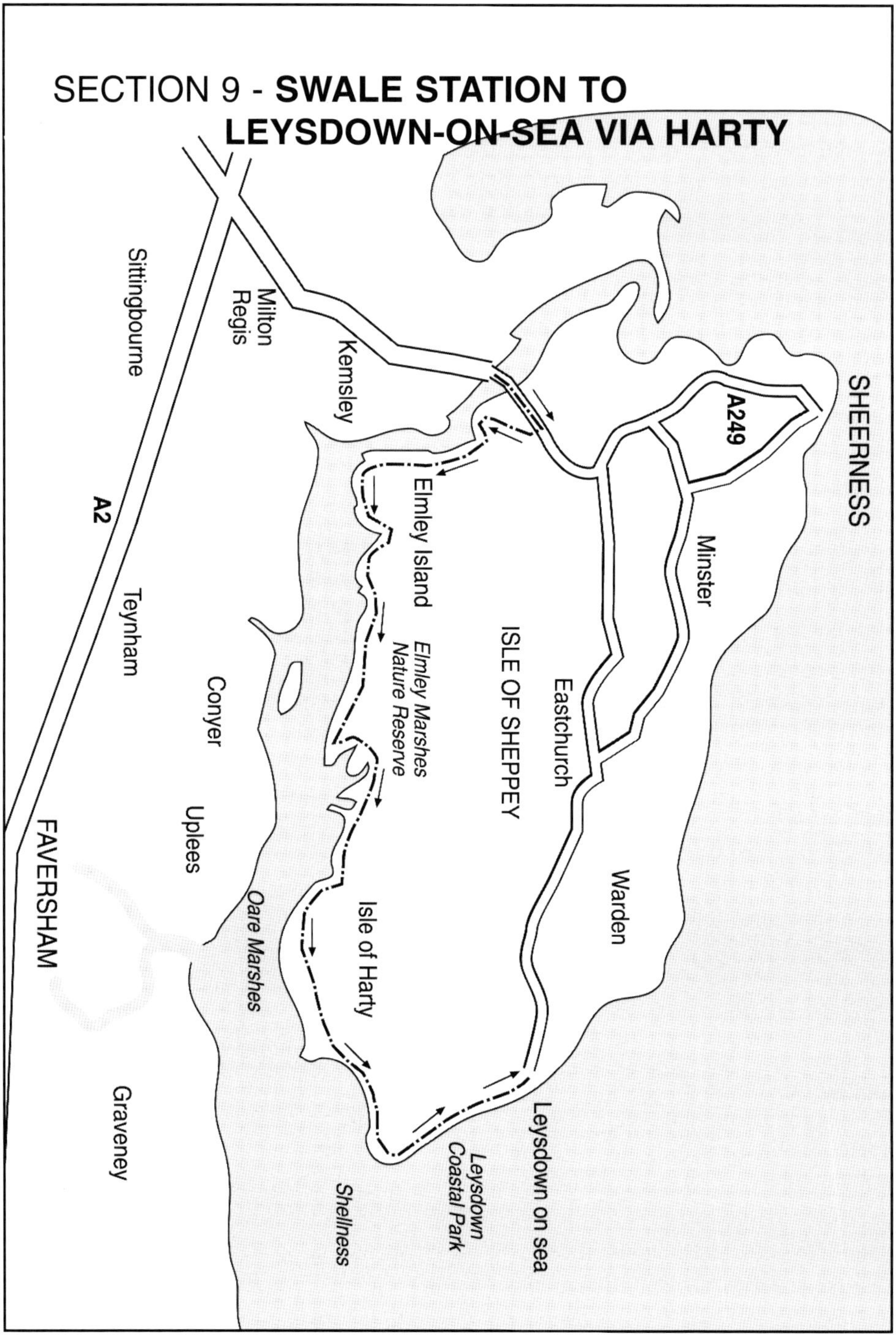

SECTION 9 - **SWALE STATION TO LEYSDOWN-ON-SEA VIA HARTY**

Distance:	15 miles.
Route:	Swale Station - Elmley Hills - Elmley Marshes - Spitend Hide - Windmill Creek - Harty - Hamlet of Shellness - Leysdown-on-Sea.
Map:	OS Explorer Sheet 149.
Public Transport:	Excellent, regular rail service linking Swale with Sheerness, Sittingbourne and the London main line. Regular bus services (not Sundays) between Leysdown-on-Sea and Sheerness.
Conditions:	This is generally very straightforward easy estuaryside (and near the end proper coastal) walking in amazingly quiet unspoilt surroundings and with quite majestic views both across Sheppey and the mainland, with Leysdown itself the only eyesore. It should be noted that there is no designated right of way alongside the Swale between Windmill Creek and the Harty Ferry Inn although no apparent difficulty of access at the time of writing. Should this change, this section will prove a good deal lengthier.
Refreshments:	See Appendix.

The first question to consider is whether to include Sheppey in your itinerary. You could choose simply to miss it and forge on towards Rainham and Rochester, perhaps ending your day's walk from Faversham at Sittingbourne and splitting the 23-mile walk on to Rochester into two with a stopover at Rainham. However the journey round Sheppey is highly recommended. The Isle of Sheppey, literally "the island where sheep are kept," is part of Kent, so if you want to say you have walked the whole of the Kent coast you really need to incorporate it into your journey, but perhaps more pertinently it offers the one and only section of true seaside walking on the Kent coast pilgrimage between Whitstable and journey's end at Dartford. It will take you two days to complete the task, but in those two days you will encounter a fantastic variety of estuaryside and seaside walking, lots of history and plenty of refreshment opportunities. It is well worth the extra legwork!

If you are continuing straight on from the end of the previous section, you need to head up to the road from the tunnel asterisked in the final paragraph of the description of that section above, using the steps and barrier as stated in that paragraph. If (as is more likely) you are starting afresh having just left a train at Swale Station, make your way down the slipway to the adjacent road. However you have reached the road, get on to the right (east) side of the road and now walk beside it across the bridge over the Swale watercourse, taking immense care. (Note that this road, although classified as the A249 at the time of writing, is being declassified now the new bridge, referred to in the previous section, is open.) Exasperatingly, once over the bridge, you can see your path heading off south-eastwards towards Elmley Marshes on the first leg of your anti-clockwise walk round Sheppey, but you cannot access it directly from here because the railway line is in the way. You are faced with a detour of over a mile! Please do not even think about trying to take a short cut over the railway line; you would be breaking the law and putting yourself at enormous risk. Gritting your teeth, proceed on beside the road and follow it, passing a lake which is to your right, and taking the first turning to the right, a track known as Ferry Road. When the track forks by some buildings, take the right fork and now trudge back towards the Swale, arriving probably some 30-40 minutes after you started, having made about 30-40 seconds' worth of progress south-eastwards. It is no doubt good for the soul, but rather less good for your feet and your shoe leather. When the road peters out, simply go forward to join the signed public footpath, bearing left and now heading south-eastwards along the path beside the Swale, with Ridham Dock, which you passed at the end of the previous section, directly opposite. At last you are properly on your way.

The going is now very easy and straightforward, the path well defined and the scenery most interesting, with views across a broad swathe of the Isle of Sheppey to your left and the Swale to your right. Ahead of you but on the opposite bank you can clearly see the Kemsley paper mill you passed on the previous section, and indeed various landmarks on the mainland side will enable you to monitor your progress eastwards on the Sheppey side, such as the mouth of Milton Creek and the houses of Sittingbourne. Soon the path loops a little to pass a tiny inlet, then heads in a direction just east of south and swings briefly south-westwards to pass another mini-inlet. The path becomes less well defined, but don't worry if you lose the route; all around you is open springy grassland, and you may simply stay as close as you wish to the water's edge. Keeping to the waterside, you now come to a surprising natural feature in the form of a green hill marked on maps as Elmley Hills(sic). Although the marked right of way passes round the left side of the hill, it is recommended that you climb to the top of it, and enjoy a superb view in all directions. You are now in the heart of the Elmley Marshes Nature Reserve, run by the Royal Society For The Protection Of Birds (RSPB); covering over 3000 acres, the reserve provides a home for vast numbers of waders and wildfowl. Now simply descend to continue your waterside walk initially south-east, then in a more truly easterly direction past a trio of creeks, namely

The southern fringes of the Isle of Sheppey are remarkably thinly populated and remote. This is the view south-westwards from the prominent hilltop just west of the old Harty Ferry.

Sharfleet, Cockleshell and Wellmarsh. With Ridham Dock and Kemsley paper mill behind you, the whole scene is very much less industrial and more pastoral, and will remain so all the way round to Sheerness.

The going remains easy and soon you have an apparent a choice of paths: there is either the embankment path on top of the sea wall or a parallel path just below the sea wall to your left. Neither are marked on maps as rights of way, but whereas the path below the sea wall is in fact available for public use, with signposts giving distances to certain landmarks ahead, signs ask you not to walk along the top of the sea wall so as to avoid disturbing nesting birds. This is undoubtedly frustrating, as the sea wall gives the best views and is the best indicator of progress back towards the sea. I can only say that if you choose to follow it, you do so at your own risk, and that of the local wildlife. Assuming you stick to the "legitimate" parallel path, simply follow the signs for Spitend Hide, keeping Spitend Marshes to your left. This is a fascinating and timeless landscape with its mixture of lush grassland and seemingly endless bands and pools of water. It can feel extraordinarily quiet; I walked this section on a fine Saturday morning in late April and did not pass a single walker. At length, at Spitend Point, you reach the wooden observation hut of Spitend Hide, and both the sea wall and the parallel path are forced to do a hairpin bend as Windmill Creek lies directly ahead. Keeping to the lower path, you pass through a gate and proceed north-westwards, then in a few hundred yards pass through a second gate, rising to meet a footpath which has followed a more inland course but has kept roughly parallel with the route described above, all the way from Sharfleet Creek. Should either of the two gates just negotiated be locked and/or insurmountable, you will need to backtrack and find a way on to this more inland footpath to reach this point.

Assuming all is well, bear right on to the path, a quite wide stony track, and head eastwards across Windmill Creek, then swing right and walk briefly parallel with the creek. The track then swings sharp left* towards Great and Little Bells. At the point where the track swings left, the approved route bears right very briefly up a gentle grassy bank to a green embankment path and turns left on to this path. Following the path, you then snake round the eastern side of Windmill Creek and the Swale end of Bells Creek; again a parallel path is available to the left should you have qualms about walking on the sea wall. You need to drop down to the parallel path as you swing round Bells Creek, to proceed through a gate close to a track that leads north-westwards to Great and Little Bells, but having negotiated that, it is plain sailing eastwards either along the embankment or parallel to it down to the left. Ahead of you is a hillside, and at length the embankment and parallel path both give out, with just one green track proceeding ahead up the hill. As you reach the top of the hill, a track forks off to the right, leading to a triangulation point from which on a clear day there is an absolutely superb view across the whole of the terrain you have covered on this section so far. The new bridge crossing over the Swale and the Kemsley paper mill are both clearly visible, and you should also now be able to pick out the tower of the parish church at

The Harty Ferry Inn, a hugely popular pub on the Isle of Sheppey named after the nearby ferry across the Swale that used to provide a link with the mainland near Faversham. The journey by road between the pub and Faversham is nearly 30 miles!

Faversham that is more or less directly across the Swale from here. Access onwards from the triangulation point is not possible so return to the fork and continue briefly eastwards, reaching the edge of a field; don't cross the field but turn left along a green field-edge path, keeping a delightful pond to your left with the buildings of Mocketts now just ahead of you. Shortly before you reach Mocketts, the path swings right, meeting a path that has come down from Leysdown Road via Harty Ferry Road**. Now walk eastwards in front of the buildings of Mocketts, going forward to join a track which soon meets a road; at the junction with the road, turn sharp right on to a footpath going down the left hand edge of a field, arriving at a stile. Cross the stile into a second field, following the direction of the arrow, and drop down to another stile, crossing it to arrive at the bottom end of Harty Ferry Road. Turn hard left on to this lane and walk north-eastwards up it, soon reaching the Harty Ferry Inn; its name is a reminder of the ferry that used to operate between here and the south side of the Swale near Faversham, a journey of one mile compared with 27 miles by road. The inn is the first refreshment opportunity on this section and you would have to be very strong-minded to pass it by. To access it, simply bear left off the lane and through the car park; if it's a fine day, you can enjoy sitting in the pub garden looking out across the Swale to the mouth of Oare Creek, an absurdly short distance away if only the ferry were still operating! (NOTE: although at the time of writing there was no difficulty of forward waterside access eastwards beyond the single-asterisked point in this paragraph, it is not designated on maps as a right of way. Should this be blocked off in future, you will be forced to follow the track on to Great and Little Bells, taking a path running north-eastwards from there to join a track taking you to Leysdown Road B2231 just east of Eastchurch. Bear right on to this road then second right along Harty Ferry Road; as this swings eastwards at Capel Gate, continue southwards along a footpath which meets the optimum route described in the above paragraph at the point that is *double*-asterisked. This inland detour is likely to add as much as two extra hours to your journey.)

Assuming you have enjoyed a pint at the Harty Ferry Inn, walk back through the pub car park and turn left back on to the lane, continuing up it north-eastwards for a few yards and very soon arriving at a signed footpath going off to the right through a field. The path isn't too clear through the field but walk through it diagonally, aiming for two parallel lines of fencing between which the path goes to exit the field and enter another field. The going is even less clear through this one, but again follow a diagonal north-easterly course uphill towards an opening at the top right-hand end, and from there simply go forward to meet the road at the hamlet of Sayes Court, aiming for the footpath sign pointing back towards you! Turn right on to the road and follow it eastwards. You soon pass the beautiful Norman church of St Thomas which is well worth visiting: described by Pevsner as the remotest church in Kent, its most notable feature is a 14th century chest with a carving on the front panel depicting a pair of jousting knights and their squires. Continuing on along the road, you drop down

A strong candidate for the prettiest and remotest church in Kent: the Norman church of St Thomas, near the Harty Ferry Inn on the Isle of Sheppey.

slightly, then when the road bends left, follow it round and soon arrive at a signed track going off to the right proclaiming that Leysdown-on-Sea, the end of this section, is four and a half miles away. They are in fact very easy miles with no logistical or route-finding problems. Follow this track in a south-easterly direction towards the water, and in a few hundred yards you reach a more open grassy area and a signed footpath going off to the left. Turn left now to follow this path.

This is absolutely superb walking: you have the wonderful prospect of the open sea ahead of you, and on a clear day there are views to Whitstable and Herne Bay. The green embankment path is well defined and you can enjoy an excellent march, looking ahead to the cottages of the Hamlet of Shellness and the Shell Ness Nature Reserve, the most easterly part of Sheppey. You approach the cottages, descending off the embankment to cross Shellness Road and going forward to arrive at the foreshore just to the left of the cottages. You are now back beside the open sea for the first time since Seasalter just west of Whitstable. The views to the north Kent coast just get better and better, and if you are lucky you may spot the towers of Reculver just east of Herne Bay. As you turn north-westwards to begin walking towards Leysdown-on-Sea, you now have a choice: you could walk along the sands, although the sands can be very soft and muddy, or else you could opt for the back of the beach or indeed the roadside. Note that a short distance along from the cottages towards Leysdown is a nudist beach, where for perhaps the only time on your walk you may feel rather overdressed. Beyond the nudist beach the going gets easier and soon you reach a proper promenade. Especially on fine days, you may find yourself in the company of quite a number of other visitors, in stark contrast to the amazing solitude further west of the Harty Ferry Inn. This is serious holiday country, and indeed as you approach the buildings of Leysdown you will find your way forward blocked by a caravan park; you are thus forced to veer left across an area of grass and a parking area to join the road, turning right to follow it into the village centre. Leysdown-on-Sea is the principal resort of Sheppey and you will find all the amenities you need here, including bus links to Sheerness where you can pick up a train back to the mainland. The section ends in the village centre at the junction of the street you have been following with the Promenade.

Leysdown-on-Sea

Described by Spence as a "wilderness of holiday camps, chalets and caravan sites," Leysdown-on-Sea is one of the most unappealing settlements you will pass through on your coastal pilgrimage. There was at one time a suggestion that it be renamed Leysdown-super-Mare, which would seem almost absurdly pretentious today given its unashamedly tacky atmosphere. It does, however, have one interesting association: in 1909, at Shell Beach close to the village, Lord Brabazon, one of the pioneers of aviation, became the first British pilot to carry out a circular flight. Between 1901 and 1950 a light railway connected Leysdown-on-Sea with Queenborough, the second town of Sheppey.

SECTION 10 - **LEYSDOWN-ON-SEA TO SWALE STATION VIA SHEERNESS**

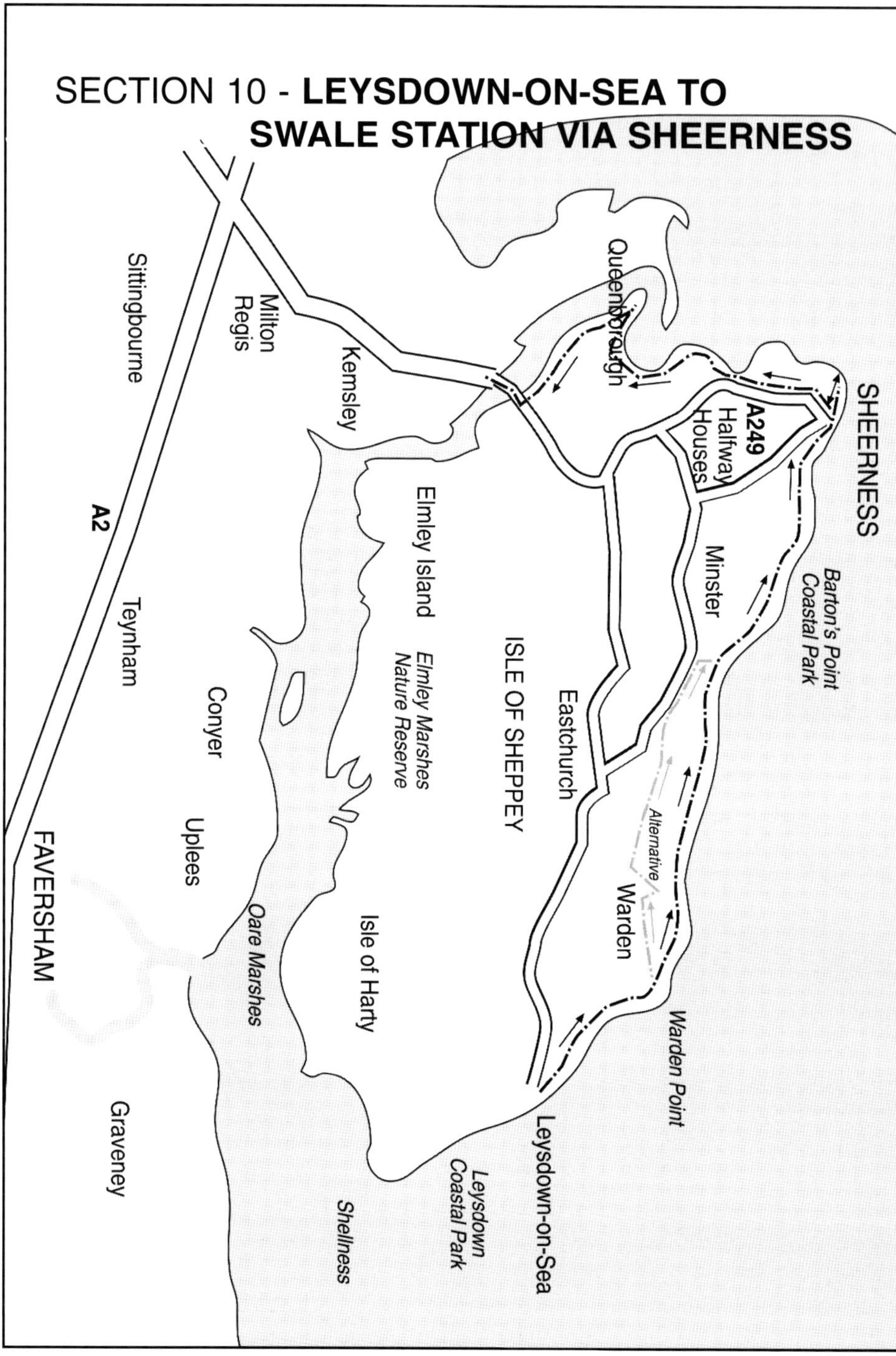

SECTION 10 - **LEYSDOWN-ON-SEA TO SWALE STATION VIA SHEERNESS**

Distance:	12 miles.
Route:	Leysdown - Warden Point - Minster - Sheerness - Queenborough - Rushenden Marshes - Swale.
Map:	OS Explorer Sheet 149.
Public Transport:	As Section 9.
Conditions:	This is a disjointed and fiddly section, but although uninspiring at times, it is full of variety and interest. It does however contain one or two potential difficulties with much depending on future cliff erosion and land use which this book cannot predict. There is also a fundamental difficulty over the first few miles depending on the state of the tides. Please read the text carefully and be prepared to change your plans if necessary.
Refreshments:	See Appendix.

The start of this rather messy section is straightforward enough, as you head back to the seafront at Leysdown-on-Sea via a street called The Promenade. This is a hugely popular street with visitors, crammed with amusement arcades, and many walkers will be only too pleased to get away from it as quickly as possible. Once on the seafront, turn left to follow the promenade proper, then on reaching a double gate, when the main walkway turns inland, drop down a slipway to follow a clear but rougher path along the shore. It is good to be away from the crowds again. Now head towards the mainly residential village of Warden; as you approach the houses, you rise slightly to meet another concrete promenade*, and it is now decision time.

Ahead of you the promenade continues for a few hundred yards, then peters out. Beyond the promenade is a mixture of rocks, stones and patches of sand which do not in themselves pose any problems for the walker; at low tide or during periods of neap tide, it will be possible for you to follow the shore via Warden Point all the way to Minster, some four and a half miles away, and this indeed is the approved route. However, during high spring tides the whole shoreline will be submerged, and therefore before you embark on this walk, YOU MUST ASCERTAIN THE STATE OF THE TIDE. Tide tables should be available from local tourist information centres and stationers' shops or on the Internet, and using this information you are strongly advised to plan your walk to coincide with a low and/or neap tide. If you haven't been able to do this IT IS ESSENTIAL TO CHECK AT LEYSDOWN-ON-SEA AS TO WHETHER THE SHORE WILL BE PASSABLE AT HIGH TIDE. SHOULD YOU FIND YOURSELF CUT OFF BY A HIGH SPRING TIDE YOU COULD PLACE YOURSELF IN SEVERE DANGER AS THERE ARE ONLY VERY LIMITED POSSIBILITIES FOR ESCAPE. Far better to wait until the tide recedes even if you have to sit it out for a couple of hours or more; if you are unprepared to do that, you will need to refer to the alternative route below. High tides are not the only hazard along the shore walk. As you undertake it you will see the frightening amount of cliff slips which have devastated the cliffs to your left - no less than two parish churches hereabouts have been lost to the sea - and one cannot rule out the possibility that parts of the foreshore which are now passable at even a high neap tide could be obliterated. Watch for local announcements and notices, and be prepared to take the alternative route set out below if you need.

If all is well, you can proceed to Minster along the shore with confidence. In some ways it is all rather reminiscent of the very first part of your Kent coast walk from Jury's Gap to Dungeness; with the cliffs to your left, there are no obvious landmarks to tell you where you are or how you are progressing, and throughout you have the open sea immediately to your right. You will notice that the number of cliff slips throughout this walk provide some almost macabre cliff formations. Not far from the start of the walk you pass two massive stone air raid shelters which have been thrown down on to the beach from the cliffs - one can only hope nobody was standing anywhere near them when they fell! - and as stated above, further slips can't be ruled out. Although you need to take care not to stumble on the uneven surfaces, the walking is not really particularly difficult or arduous, and in good weather you should really enjoy the unspoilt surroundings and views which extend out towards the south Essex coast. You are unlikely to be on your own, especially on fine weekends or in summer, since this is popular country for beachcombers and fishermen. In due course, not far beyond the barely identifiable Royal Oak Point, you will notice a concrete promenade starting to your left, which you access by means of quite a tough scramble across the shingle. The start of the promenade** signals your approach to the sprawling village of Minster, and it is now a straightforward walk along the promenade with housing to your left.

The alternative route is sadly a lot less enjoyable, as it involves road walking throughout with no sea views, there being no path, nor possibility of access, along the present cliff edge. Having hit the concrete promenade at Warden that is single-asterisked in the first descriptive paragraph in this section, you will shortly see a car park and a flight of steps leading up to Imperial Drive. Follow Imperial Drive up to the T-junction with Thorn Hill Road, turning right into this road and following it north-westwards to another T-junction, here+ turning left into Warden Road. Walk westwards along Warden Road, which shortly beyond a pub swings sharp right then

Although owing to erosion there is no continuous cliff path between Leysdown-on-Sea and Minster, limited access to the cliffs is possible. This is the fine view back to Leysdown-on-Sea from above the village of Warden.

shortly sharp left, now heading south-westwards to pass a large holiday complex. Beyond the complex the road swings to the right to reach a T-junction with Plough Road; turn right into this road, going forward to reach a T-junction with a road coming in hard from the left. Turn right into this road, marked on maps as Chequers Road, and go forward into Chapel Street, now almost in the centre of Minster. Look out for a church to your left and opposite this church turn right into Baldwin Road, going forward to a path which brings you down to the start of the promenade that is double-asterisked in the above paragraph. (NOTE: There is, at the time of writing, a path leading off to the right from the bottom of Imperial Drive mentioned at the start of this paragraph, going uphill on to the cliffs; the path enters an area of woodland then goes forward to the right of a caravan park and on to the sea end of Warden Road. Simply follow Warden Road westwards, being reunited with the principal alternative route at + above. The cliff walk is dramatic, providing superb views back to Leysdown-on-Sea and the north Kent coast, and if you have time there's no reason why you couldn't undertake it as a detour and then return to the shore to follow the main route. HOWEVER, THIS CLIFF WALK IS EXTREMELY DANGEROUS IN PLACES. Cliff slips have reduced the path to just a few inches wide at times, and it is very possible that by the time you come to walk this section it will either have been closed down, or fallen into the sea. IF IN DOUBT, TURN BACK, AND USE THE SAFE ALTERNATIVE ROUTE.)

Whichever route you have followed from Warden, continue along the promenade towards Minster. In due course you see a road named the Leas joining you to the left and running parallel with the promenade, and you will see that this road reaches a junction with The Broadway which goes off to the left. A little way along The Broadway to the right is first a useful pub and then a large hotel; The Broadway itself travels south to reach Minster's village street although as this is a good mile away from the sea front, you may wish to plough on towards Sheerness. If you do have time to make the detour, you will in the old part of inland Minster find one real gem. In around 670 AD a nunnery was founded here by St Sexburga, widow of a Saxon king of Kent, and although the nunnery was destroyed by the Danes, it was rebuilt early in the 12th century to include an abbey church. This incorporated some of the earlier Saxon building, making it one of the oldest centres of worship in the country, and a parish church was added in the 13th century to create effectively a double church. There are some very fine monuments in the church including a canopied tomb of Robert de Shurland, a former Lord Warden of the Cinque Ports, incorporating an effigy of his horse which is said to have carried him out into the estuary to seek a pardon from Edward I following his murder of a priest. There are also two huge brasses including one of Joan, Lady Northwood which dates back to around 1330 and is said to be among the earliest female brasses in England.

Beyond The Broadway, keep walking along the promenade which becomes a shingle bank, but even the shingle provides quite easy going underfoot. Almost before you know it, you are back on concrete again, and quite imperceptibly you find yourself moving into Sheerness, the principal town of Sheppey. Your introduction to the town is hardly very inspiring, with dreary rows of houses strung along the coast road to your left, and you may prefer to keep your eyes fixed on the sea; Sheerness is a busy port and ferry terminal and you may see a number of large seagoing vessels entering or leaving port. You pass an extremely prominent church then continue past two easily accessible refreshment possibilities, McDonalds and the massive Tesco superstore. It is possible for you to continue for just over a quarter of a mile beyond Tesco along the promenade, but tantalisingly, just a stone's throw from Garrison Point, the north-western tip of Sheppey, you reach a dead end and are forced back. It is necessary for you to backtrack almost all the way to Tesco, but just before you reach the car park, look out for a lake to your right (inland side of the promenade) and turn right on to the path following the left (east) side of the lake. Soon you reach a main road at a roundabout. This is the nearest you get to the town centre of Sheerness, accessible to your left, although you need to turn right to continue the walk.

Sheerness

The principal town of Sheppey, Sheerness stands at a key strategic point at the mouth of the Medway. In 1547 a gun battery was established at Garrison Point (see above) to guard the river, but in 1667 the defences were breached by the Dutch admiral de Ruyter. Two years later a strong fortress was built here, and in the 19th century it became a dockyard town, the naval dockyard surviving until 1960; there was at one time a naval coaling station here which saved the new steam-powered vessels the trouble of negotiating the Medway down to Chatham. The town itself contains virtually nothing of any architectural interest, Pevsner going as far as to say that of its secular buildings, "none is good and most are exceedingly bad." The lofty 19th century Roman Catholic church of St Henry and St Elizabeth is however regarded as one of the better creations of E.W.Pugin, and there is a clock tower that was built to celebrate the coronation of Edward VII. The 19th century dockyard, designed in 1812, is more interesting: although some demolition has gone on, many of the most important original buildings remain including the three-storied Captain's House, the (now redundant) Garrison Church with its very grand Ionic portico, and the yard's boatstore which is a very early example of a multi-storey iron-framed building. Unfortunately, the dock area is out of bounds unless you have a visitor's pass or legitimate business there, and casual visitors are not allowed. The dockyard now accommodates a busy container and passenger port, with a ferry service to Flushing (Vlissingen) in the Netherlands, and also a big industrial estate.

The town is associated with two famous figures of the past: the body of Lord Nelson was brought by sea to Sheerness in a barrel of spirit after the Battle of Trafalgar, and the actor Edmund Kean began his acting career here at the age of 15.

As stated, turn right at the roundabout off the lakeside path to follow the main road, almost immediately arriving at another roundabout. The first exit is the road to the out-of-bounds Sheerness Docks (see above); the way forward is the second exit off the roundabout, High Street, and you follow this road with the high walls of the dockyard towering above you to your right. You are now proceeding through the Blue Town area of Sheerness. Formerly known as Blue Houses, it gets its name from the timbered cabins that were built by dockyard workmen in open places round the docks in the late

For those in peril on the sea....this church is one of the most conspicuous features of the seafront at Sheerness, a busy freight and passenger port.

The Red Lion in the High Street, Blue Town, a part of Sheerness that was once known as Blue Houses. The name is derived from timbered cabins that were built hereabouts by dockyard workers and painted with grey and blue naval paint.

18th century, and were painted with grey and blue naval paint. At the far end of High Street swing left into West Street to arrive back at the main road. Turn right to follow it, keeping to the pavement. You need to keep to the section of pavement closest to the fencing on the right hand (west) side, with a vast car pound on the other side of the fence. Shortly this concrete walkway, keeping the fenced car pound immediately to the right, veers away to the right of the road and proceeds south-westwards. This is somewhat surreal walking, with high stone walls to your left and formidable fencing to your right, but soon you arrive at the water's edge once more. However, this is not the open sea: you have effectively rounded Garrison Point and are now looking out across the Medway at its confluence with the north-western end of the Swale. This is your first view of the Medway, which will be your companion for large parts of the next two sections. Continue along the waterside path, beside the top end of the Swale; the views from here are magnificent, including not only the Swale but the Medway estuary and the Isle of Grain with its massive power station. Soon you arrive at the little town of Queenborough, turning left immediately opposite the Hard into the High Street.

Queenborough

The town was named after Queen Philippa of Hainault, wife of Edward III, during whose reign in the 14th century the town received its charter. It was established to provide a defence against French raids, the Swale on which Queenborough stands being the usual route for shipping at that time, and indeed a castle was built here between 1361 and 1377. It became an important centre of the wool trade in the Middle Ages, and although it was to decline in importance over the years - its pubs these days no longer throng with the Medway bargees as it once did - it has latterly boasted a deep water port, a ferrous sulphate factory and engineering and pharmaceutical factories. At one time there was a ferry link between the town and Holland. Its name was taken in vain in a play written by Thomas Middleton in the early 17th century entitled The Mayor Of Queenborough, satirising the presumptiousness of towns such as this one which continued to elect mayors even though they had shrunk to mere villages. The castle has long gone, having been demolished by Oliver Cromwell's forces in the 17th century - ironically shortly before a successful Dutch raid! - but there are still some very appealing aspects to the town, including its tiny harbour (see below), its attractive quayside and a High Street that boasts two outstanding buildings, the Guildhall and Holy Trinity Church. The Guildhall dates back to 1793 and has an impressive three-bay front of yellow brick with Tuscan columns, while the church dates back to the 14th century and boasts a tower that belonged to an earlier Norman structure. It has a superb late 17th century painted ceiling depicting the sounding of the Last Trump by the Angel of the Apocalypse, a font dating back to 1610 with carvings representing the castle, then still standing, and a churchyard that is crammed with tombs, mostly of seafarers. The greatest of the tombs is that to the Greet family, with its baroque chest rising to a finial and obelisk: Simon Jenkins describes it as a "fine memorial to a once-royal port."

Follow the High Street eastwards. It is worth detouring hard right into South Street to enjoy a stroll along the quayside; the compact little harbour here, packed with boats, has something of a Cornish flavour. Return to the High Street and continue to its junction with the main village street, the B2007, then turn right to follow the street briefly - the station is just across the road - and turn right again into Rushenden Road. Follow the road, crossing over the creek and going forward to the Klondyke Park industrial estate which is a short way beyond. Unfortunately the right of way shown on some maps as running immediately beside the creek up the east edge of the industrial estate has been extinguished. You need to pass the main gate to the estate and just beyond the estate look for a track that leads off to the right, taking you down to the waterside. Turn left to follow a good waterside embankment path. (NB The access track to here from the Klondyke estate isn't a designated right of way although at the time of writing there was no difficulty of access; were this to become unavailable for any reason, you could continue along Rushenden Road to the point where it is crossed by an old industrial railway and turn right along a right of way immediately beside the old railway to arrive at the point single-asterisked below. You could then effectively detour back towards the Klondyke estate along the waterside path.) Shortly you reach the old industrial railway coming in from the left, and you are forced to drop down off the embankment and across the railway* to join a path that continues alongside the Swale, heading initially just south of west and then swinging north-westwards. In due course you reach the entrance to some rather bleak-looking industrial workings**.

Ahead of you, immediately beyond the workings, is Ladies Hole Point, where the Swale describes an enormous loop, and indeed if you mount the slight incline to the left of the track you are on, you will from the top of the bank see the loop clearly and get a fine panorama of the Tailness Marshes and the Medway Estuary on the other side of the Swale. Then, looking to your left, you will see the Swale as it heads in a south-easterly direction, with the Kings Ferry Bridge, where you are to complete your circle, just a mile and a half distant. There is no designated right of way alongside the Swale between where you are standing and the Kings Ferry Bridge; nonetheless there is a track available, and to find it it is necessary to turn south-eastwards and proceed along the top of the bank, picking up the well-defined track which now continues without obstruction or apparent prohibition all the way back to the Kings Ferry Bridge. You have the Swale for company throughout, with views over the Swale to the Chetney Marshes - a very important site for nesting birds - to your right, and the rather less aesthetically pleasing sewage works and modern housing of Rushenden to your left. At the end you scramble up to the road, turn right and cross the bridge, then immediately on returning to the "mainland" you will see the Swale station entrance on the left. To access the next section, climb over the metal barrier on the right just before the station entrance to reach the steps that take you down to reunite you with the Saxon Shore Way and the start of the next section of walking.

As stated, however, the whole of the section beside the Swale described in the above paragraph is not a designated right of way and it is possible that land use may change and/or access along the track may be barred in future. The most obvious alternative route according to current maps would seem to be to backtrack from the entrance to the industrial workings at the point double-asterisked above to Rushenden Road, turn right on to that road and follow it briefly, then turn left into Cullet Drive, following it to the very end. At the end of Cullet Drive turn right into Argent Road, and at the end of Argent Road turn left to join a path that proceeds south-east by Joan Fleet to the White House, and then on southwards to join the road just before Kings Ferry Bridge. Turn right to follow the road to the bridge. However, because of the construction of the new bridge, the section of path from the White House southwards is shut at the time of writing with no guarantee when or if it will ever reopen. If the walk beside the Swale is unavailable, you may prefer to cut your losses and simply return to Queenborough Station and join one of the regular trains back to Swale Station; if you can't bear to do that, the last resort would be to continue past the station entrance walking eastwards along Main Road (B2007) to a roundabout, here turning right on to the A249 and following it south-eastwards. At the next roundabout, with the B2231, bear right along Sheppey Way (A249 up to the time of the new bridge opening) and continue along the old main road to the old bridge crossing.

PLEASE REMEMBER: RIGHTS OF WAY IN THIS AREA MAY BE SIGNIFICANTLY AFFECTED BY THE WORKS RELATING TO THE OPENING OF THE NEW BRIDGE CROSSING. YOU ARE ADVISED TO MAKE ENQUIRY LOCALLY BEFORE COMMITTING YOURSELF TO A PARTICULAR ROUTE, AND BE PREPARED TO BE FLEXIBLE IN YOUR PLANS.

The old bridge crossing of the Swale.

SECTION 11 - **SWALE STATION TO ROCHESTER**

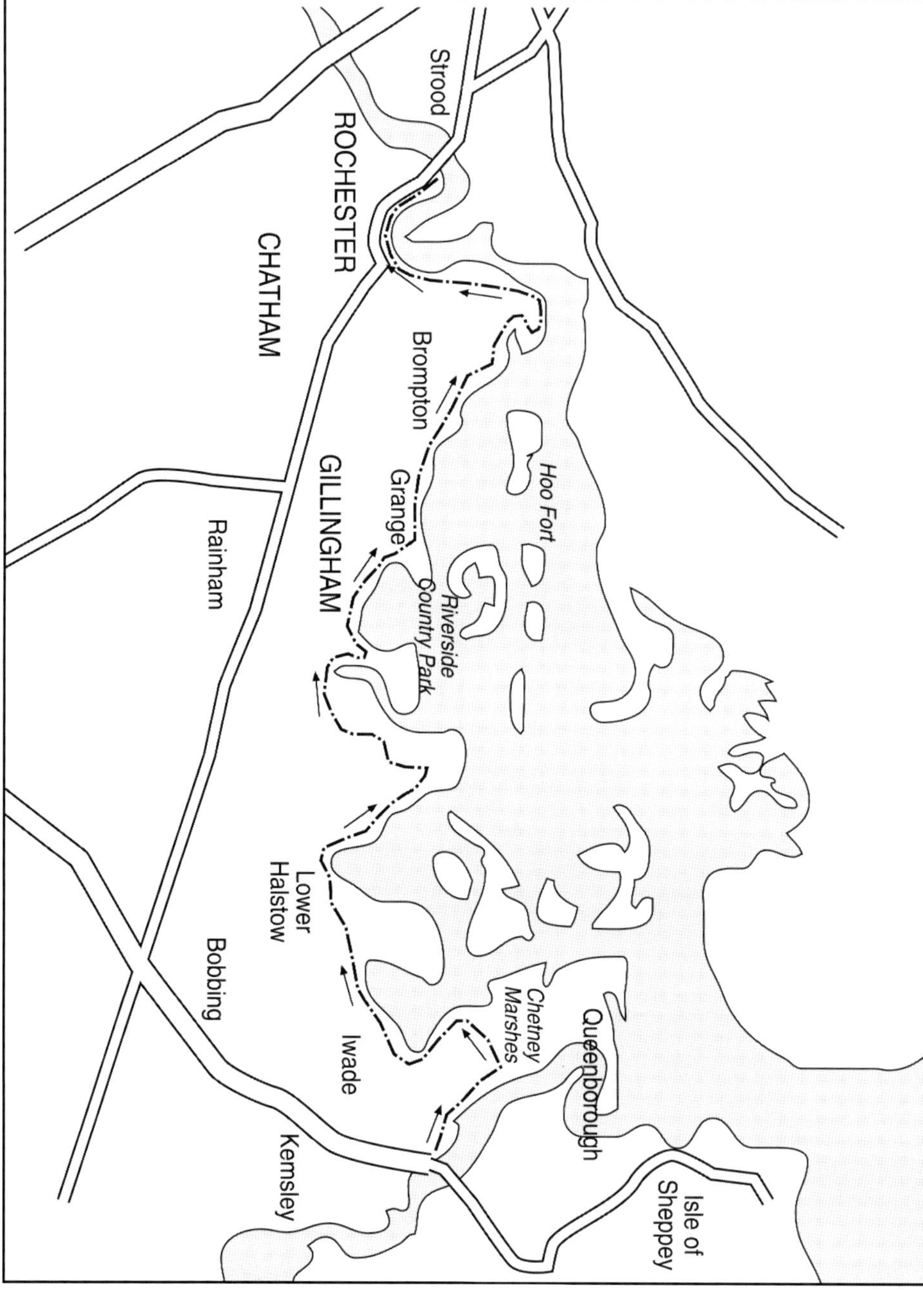

SECTION 11 - **SWALE STATION TO ROCHESTER**

Distance:	18 miles.
Route:	Swale Station - Raspberry Hill - Lower Halstow - Upchurch - Rainham - Strand - Gillingham - St Mary's Island - Chatham - Rochester.
Maps:	OS Explorer Sheets 149 and 163.
Public Transport:	Excellent, regular rail service linking Swale with Sittingbourne and the London main line. Two fast and two slow trains each hour most days linking Rainham, Gillingham, Chatham and Rochester with London Victoria and Faversham, and a further two trains an hour from Gillingham, Chatham and Rochester to London Charing Cross.
Conditions:	This section is thankfully straightforward and very easy, with none of the logistical problems of the previous one. Although it is a long section, it could conveniently be split in half with a break at Rainham, whose railway station is just fifteen minutes' walk from the shoreline. The split option may be preferred if you wish to take half a day off to enjoy the many attractions of Chatham and Rochester, and you are not too impatient to get back to the coastline proper! There is some fantastic birdwatching country along this section so don't forget your binoculars.
Refreshments:	See Appendix.

The section starts at the foot of the steps leading down from the road roughly opposite the entrance to Swale Station; if you have just completed the Sheppey circuit or are joining the walk following a rail journey to the station at Swale you will have descended the steps, whereas if you are continuing straight on from Sittingbourne using the walking route described in section 8, you will just have passed under the short rail/road tunnel. Proceed from the foot of the steps briefly along the metalled road westwards away from the bridge, but almost immediately turn right to rejoin the embankment path that now forges on up the south side of the Swale estuary, following the course of the Saxon Shore Way. The scene to your left is now much more open and

One of the loveliest spots on the long trek from Swale to Rochester: the church of St Margaret, Lower Halstow, which dates back to Saxon times and is the gateway to a lovely walk alongside Halstow Creek.

pastoral, although the view to Sheppey to your right is somewhat marred by the sight of the sewage works and modern housing of Rushenden. The walking is easy and enjoyable, but after a mile and a half or so further Swale-side progress is halted by a gate and "Keep Out" signs; the area beyond, the Chetney Marshes, is an important nesting site for birds and public access is not permitted. You are forced to swing sharply south-west, and to bid a permanent farewell to the Swale. From the gate you can just perceive the Swale swinging sharply right, en route to its meeting with the Medway a little above Queenborough which you'll have observed if you have included Sheppey in your journey. You should also be able to observe the massive tower of Grain power station, although this is still two good days' walking away.

It is disappointing to lose sight of the water as you head south-westwards away from the Swale, but the path, continuing to follow the Saxon Shore Way, is well defined and there is a good open and remote feel to the walking. Further signs warn you to keep away from the nesting areas, underlining the importance of this area as a haven for a rich variety of birds including avocet, shelduck, gadwall and pochard. You cross a metalled farm road and continue on, soon arriving at the side of one of many little inlets that branch off the Medway estuary; the northern part of this marshy inlet consists of a channel called the Shade, flowing from Funton Creek, and the path swings right to follow the east side of the inlet. This is lovely walking, with excellent views towards the Medway whose estuary and its offshoots you will be following all the way to Rochester. Bird life is plentiful and varied, so keep the binoculars handy. Ahead of you, as you proceed south-eastwards beside the marshes, is a small hill, picturesquely named Raspberry Hill; the path does not keep to the side of the marsh round the foot of the hill, but continues in a south-easterly direction and climbs the hill. As you climb, you become aware of a field boundary just to your left, and it is necessary to transfer to and follow the left side of the field boundary (the signposting is not terribly clear) to access the exit at the top. Pause to admire the extensive views, then, ignoring the Saxon Shore Way signpost, turn right on to Raspberry Hill Lane and follow the lane south-westwards all the way to the village of Lower Halstow, two miles distant. This is one of the longer stretches of road walking you will have to endure on your Kent coastal walk, but in fact it is quite agreeable, with not a huge amount of traffic and good views initially to the inlet which lies to your right. Beyond the inlet is the Barksore Marshes peninsula, which is inaccessible for walkers, and it is only once you have passed the hamlet of Great Barksore and reached the village of Lower Halstow that you come to the next inlet created by Twinney Creek, and are able to rejoin the waterside once more.

As you arrive in the Lower Halstow, look out for the Saxon Shore Way signpost pointing you off the road along a path towards the village church to your right. The church of St Margaret dates back to Saxon times, boasting a Norman font, a complete Saxon nave and chancel, some medieval wall paintings and a Jacobean pulpit. Pass just to the left of the church and then carefully follow the Saxon Shore Way markers to join an obvious embankment path that now proceeds delightfully along another mini-peninsula up the west side of the Halstow Creek inlet. The area has associations with the Romans who made bricks and gathered oysters hereabouts, and subsequently this was an important collecting point by spirit-sail barges for bricks and clay. This is superb walking, in quite delightful surroundings: there are extensive views across the inlet to Barksore Marshes and beyond, and the landscape to your left is truly rural with a mixture of marshes, fields and orchards, reminding you that you are still very much in the Garden of England! You pass the very pretty little harbour at Twinney Wharf, and continue by the waterside past Callows House to another wharf just east of the hamlet of Ham Green. At this second wharf you will note the Saxon Shore Way pointing left, along a lane away from the waterside and heading south-westwards to Ham Green. A path does, however, continue along the waterside up to the top of the peninsula, and some maps erroneously suggest a public right of way being available all the way round and along the east side of the next inlet created by Otterham Creek. But having proceeded happily along a good path to the top of the peninsula, through orchards with an abundance of apple blossom in spring, you will disappointingly find further progress blocked by a chained gate. Allow yourself a moment to enjoy the superb views across the Medway towards the Isle of Grain, then make your way back to the Saxon Shore Way as it proceeds away from the waterside along the lane to Ham Green.

As you arrive at Ham Green you reach a junction with a road; turn right and almost immediately left, following the Saxon Shore Way signposts. Proceed along the Saxon Shore Way alongside orchards, then use a rather rickety stile to turn right across the corner of a field, crossing a second stile and turning right to follow a narrow path

between an area of woodland and a farm. Go forward to arrive at a road, turning left to follow the road and in a couple of hundred yards turning right to follow a path through a field, sticking to the Saxon Shore Way. The signposting couldn't be clearer. The path becomes a lane which proceeds south-westwards to reach a road just west of the sprawling village of Upchurch, the childhood home of Sir Francis Drake. Turn right to follow the road westwards past a pub and the large Horsham Farm, then as the road swings sharp left in just under half a mile, go briefly straight on into a driveway. Having joined this driveway, bear left almost immediately as directed by the Saxon Shore Way signpost into an orchard, keeping to the left side of the orchard and following it round, then at the far top end you use a narrow path to drop down to the road again. Turn right on to the road then, just beyond the entrance to a caravan park, turn right along a lane heading for a wharf which is in fact an accumulation of industrial units at the south-west end of the Otterham Creek inlet. Barges were once built at the boatyards here, and then used to carry bricks from the nearby brickfields.
As you reach the wharf you will see a footpath going off to the left. This provides a useful short cut to Rainham, which boasts a fine church, the best variety of amenities since Sheerness (or Sittingbourne, if you missed out Sheppey) and a railway station; to reach the town centre simply follow this path to the road, turn right on to the road and then turn left at the next road junction. The station and town centre is just over half a mile away. To continue along the coast path towards Rochester, bear slightly right to pass along the left (south-west) side of the wharf, soon arriving back at the waterside again. You are now embarking on a walk along another mini-peninsula, this one separating Otterham Creek and Rainham Creek. A very pleasant walk along the west side of Otterham Creek follows on a good embankment path, but at a locked gate you are forced to turn left, down a flight of steps and over a footbridge to arrive shortly at a T-junction with a lane. Turn left to follow the lane. There is a row of houses to your right, with the modest heights of Motney Hill immediately behind, but to your left there is a good view of Otterham Creek and its eastern shore which you were of course sadly unable to follow! Walk down the road, and very shortly Rainham Creek opens up to your right, with its surrounding mudflats and channels; to the north-west of Motney Hill are important saltings and reedbeds that are maintained by the RSPB. This was once a busy shipping area, and there were three quays in operation hereabouts, with mud being brought here in spirit-sail barges from nearby marshes. You now join a path which follows the east side of the creek to the "landward" end of the peninsula; there really is a "coastal" feel to this landscape despite your distance from the open sea. As you reach the end of this little peninsula you bear right, and it is now easy and enjoyable walking beside the extensive saltmarshes and mudflats of the Medway estuary. This whole area is known as the North Kent Marshes, designated as a Site of Special Scientific Interest and an area of national and international importance for wintering waders, ducks and geese.
Shortly you arrive at the Riverside Country Park, a popular spot for residents of nearby

Rainham and Gillingham, so do not be surprised to have company. A little beyond the country park you will see an excellent wheelchair-friendly path branching off to the right up a very thin spit of land extending towards the Medway. Follow this path along the spit; although this is a detour, as you are forced back the same way you came, it is really too good to miss especially if the weather is fine. At the end of the spit is an area of trees known as Horrid Hill, taking its name from the conditions endured by French prisoners kept on hulks moored here during the Napoleonic Wars, but in fact this is a superb viewpoint, with a viewing platform, topograph and list of birds you may be fortunate enough to see here. Over 40 species are listed, from great-crested grebe to redbreasted merganser, from peregrine to oystercatcher, and although you may not be fortunate enough to see more than a tiny percentage of them on your visit, this is another spot where you will want to have the binoculars readily available. Notwithstanding the fact that the mass of towers and outbuildings of Kingsnorth Power Station immediately across the estuary is not aesthetically very appealing, this view adds to the vitality and variety of the surroundings. At one time this part of the estuary, with its islands and peninsulas surrounded by thick alluvium, provided rich pickings for clay-getters who would load their barges in between the tides.

Return now to the main path beside the Medway, and keep walking; progress continues to be straightforward although there is the less welcome prospect of the A289 Gillingham bypass now to your left, and a big industrial works straight ahead of you. Just before the works you are forced to bear left round the east side of them, but it is suggested you keep going as far round as you can along a good path, turning left

Keep right on to the end of the road....the fine embankment path which provides easy going for Saxon Shore Way and Kent coast walkers beside Otterham Creek just to the north of Rainham.

only when you have to, thus giving you excellent views across the Cinque Port Marshes to the estuary, and to the smart waterfront development a little further west. Then proceed round the east side of the works, soon reaching a T-junction with a factory approach road; turn right on to this road, going down to the forbidding entrance to another works, but just before the entrance you will see a signed path going off to the left. Follow this path past the new waterfront residential development. Immediately beyond the new housing there is a lovely old brown-painted house, named Longhope Cottage, to the left, whilst to the right is the Medway Cruising Club. Just beyond Longhope Cottage you enter the Strand Leisure Park with its lawns, miniature golf course and amusements, while directly ahead of you is the Strand Leisure Pool, a sorry-looking affair at the time of writing, with a refurbishment long overdue. Pass to the coastward side of the pool; immediately beyond it your way forward is barred by a green fence and you are forced to bear left, away from the coast, up a metalled drive, keeping a children's park to your left. Continue ahead, bearing slightly right, up the hill to reach a roundabout where you meet the very busy A289. Turn right here to follow beside the A289 along a cycle track, signposted route 1 for Chatham Maritime. (If you wish to visit the town of Gillingham, set well back from the coast, you need to cross straight over the roundabout and continue along Church Street, going forward into Ingram Road, turning right into Railway Street; the station is a short distance along this street and the town centre is immediately beyond that. This sprawling industrial town is of no real historical interest, although it was the birthplace of William Adams in 1564: the first Englishman to visit Japan, he became a Samurai warrior, and James Clavell's novel *Shogun* is based on his exploits.)

Assuming you have bypassed Gillingham and turned right at the roundabout on to the cycle track mentioned above, you must now endure a rather unpleasant walk beside the A289, keeping it to your left. At least it is safe, and there is some interest to your right, with the boat showroom of the Gillingham Marina to browse in if you have just had some luck on the Lottery, although most will probably be content to gaze through the glass! Keep ploughing along the cycle track, with the very busy A289 to your left; in due course you pass under a footbridge and find yourself walking not beside the A289 as it heads down to the Medway Tunnel, but an eastbound slip road. At the top end of the slip road you arrive at a road junction+. Unless you are in a hurry (an alternative route for those pressed for time is set out at * below) do not follow the signs for Chatham but bear right here along a quieter road, Maritime Way, with the modern housing and retail developments of Chatham Maritime close by. Ahead of you is a bridge crossing over a stretch of water incorporating a marina, on the other side of which is the remarkable St Mary's Island; you head straight for the bridge, admiring the splendid old sailing ship Julia that lies to your left. Now, using the pavement on the right (east) side, cross the bridge and then bear right immediately, dropping down to the water's edge and going through a metal gate to join a boardwalk path beside the eastern stretch of water that separates the island from the "mainland."

Follow the board walk to its end, mounting the steps and bearing sharp left to join a footpath. Almost immediately, a wider path forks right off this footpath; take this path which goes gently uphill into a pleasant grassy area, that even has a separate dog run leading off it! From the hilltop there is an excellent view over the island, with its modern housing making up the central section, and to the east a harsh industrial landscape that is strictly out of bounds for walkers. You can also enjoy looking down the Medway estuary, with views to many of the riverside features passed earlier in this section. Pass the far entrance to the dog run then follow the wide path downhill to the houses; as you reach the houses, take the path forking right which brings you to a magnificent Millennium sculpture, and just beyond that you may access the bank of the Medway and the start of the riverside walk. It is good to be back by the water's edge once more. This point, effectively the boundary on the island between the new housing and the heavy industry (which as previously stated, is a "no-go" area for walkers), is known as Finsborough Ness, and at one time there used to be a regular ferry service across the Medway from here. Although the ferry has long gone, you can enjoy what is a beautiful view across the river to the wooded hills of the Hoo Peninsula. There is a grace and elegance to the Medway at this point that reminds one a little of the Thames as it wends its way through Buckinghamshire and Berkshire towards London, and its profusion of pleasure craft underlines its popularity with the sailing fraternity. But though the scene is peaceful, an information board at the waterside reminds you that the Medway around St Mary's Island was notorious for its prison hulks in the late 18th and early 19th centuries, occupied by prisoners taken from such conflicts as the Napoleonic Wars and the American War of Independence. One example of a Medway hulk was the Brunswick, in which 460 prisoners were crammed on to a deck measuring just 125ft long and 40ft wide, with only sufficient hammock space for 431 "hung so close together that (the prisoners') irons became entangled." The food on the hulks was appalling, the menu including bread that was described as "not fit even for a dog to eat" and biscuits that were "mouldy and green on both sides." You will also learn of the privations suffered by the inmates of the prison that was once situated hereabouts, culminating in the infamous 1861 Dining Hall Riot.

Lovely walking follows as, having reached the riverside, you turn left and head westwards along the riverside path, a popular amenity for the residents of the sizeable modern housing estates that have been established on the island. Soon the magnificent Upnor Castle comes into view, dominating the scene on the other side of the Medway, and though you will have the chance to visit the castle on the next section, this is the best place to capture its full glory on camera. As you walk, you swing from westwards to southwards and the prospect becomes less pastoral and more industrial; the view eastwards across the island is uninspiring, and at the time of writing it would appear to be ripe for further development. Cross over the water using the swingbridge and now you enter a major area of industrial development, passing a large redbrick construction calling itself Pump House 5. You are able to stay close to the waterside but in due course are forced away from it on to a road known as Leviathan Way which you follow, soon reaching a roundabout. The approved route goes straight over the roundabout, but the right hand exit provides access to Chatham Dockyard, a massively interesting area and well worth a visit; the dockyard is described a little more fully under the entry devoted to Chatham below. Assuming you have detoured to the dockyard, you must retrace your steps to the roundabout to continue the approved route, going forward along Western Avenue to a roundabout junction with Dock Road. Turn right and follow this road. (* If you wish to omit St Mary's Island, turn left at the junction marked + above, following the blue signposts for Chatham, and very shortly you will arrive at the roundabout junction of Western Avenue and Dock Road. Simply go straight over this roundabout to continue, now reunited with the approved route.)

Now proceed quite steeply uphill to another roundabout, go straight over the roundabout and then descend, passing a splendid statue of Kitchener on your left. Shortly afterwards the Chatham Library appears on your right, and you join the library approach road to enter a fine riverside park; you can in fact backtrack a little downstream as far as the attractive Command Inn and Medway Heritage Centre (see below), but can go on no further, so now proceed upstream, keeping the river to your right, towards Rochester. There are splendid views to Rochester Cathedral as you proceed. You are able to follow the river as far as a jetty just beyond the Staples store that lies to your left, but there is no possibility of going further along the waterside beyond the jetty, so at this point turn left to walk past Staples and join the main road. If you wish to visit the centre of Chatham you need to turn left and backtrack to the road junction, from which the shops and other amenities of Chatham are a few yards away. Otherwise, turn right on to the main road beyond Staples and keep walking, soon passing under a railway bridge and shortly after that reaching Rochester railway station which is on your right. Go straight on beyond the station and cross over the very busy main road to enter Rochester High Street, now a pedestrian precinct crammed with lovely old houses, shops, teaplaces and restaurants - a pilgrim's paradise!

Chatham and Rochester

Because these settlements are effectively joined to one another - it really is not possible to say where one comes out of Chatham and into Rochester - it seems convenient to describe them together.

The name **Chatham** *means "homestead or village in or near a wood," a rather rural description which belies Chatham's former importance as one of Britain's leading naval towns. Undoubtedly the most significant feature of Chatham is its dockyard. It was created as a naval base by Henry VIII at a time when Chatham was merely a fishing village, and developed by Elizabeth I who established it as a Royal Dockyard; by the reign of Charles II, Chatham had become the largest naval base in England. After an attack on the docks by the Dutch in 1667, defences were strengthened, and further expansion followed during the Napoleonic Wars*

The keep of Rochester Castle, built by the then Archbishop of Canterbury at the end of the 1120's. It is over 100ft high and the largest such construction in England, with walls that are a massive 12ft thick.

including the construction of a series of forts built on a hill east of Chatham, known as the Chatham Lines. In 1765 HMS Victory, subsequently to become Lord Nelson's flagship at the Battle of Trafalgar, was launched here - one of many hundreds of ships which over four centuries originated from the yard - and throughout the 19th century it was the principal naval dockyard in England. It closed in 1984 and was converted to an industrial area, marina and museum, with part of the docks preserved as the Chatham Historic Dockyard. Of particular interest is the Ropery, the dockyard's rope-making centre and the longest brick building in the UK; the Covered Slipways, a sequence of huge roofed spaces lining the Medway; the Wooden Walls, a gallery which re-enacts the construction of an 18th century vessel but using modern display techniques; the 18th century Main Gate with its two brown towers and royal coat of arms over the entrance; the early 19th century dockyard church; the early 18th century Sail and Colour Loft, a huge workshop where the sails of the Victory were made; and the elegant Commissioner's House, built in 1704. The last warship to be built for the Navy at Chatham was the submarine Ocelot, which has been moored in a large inland dock nearby, and which can be inspected today. In its last years the dockyard served as a refitting base for nuclear submarines.

The dockyard is not the town's only attraction for visitors. The town has a strong link with Charles Dickens who lived here between 1817 and 1821 at what is now 11 Ordnance Terrace, a three-storey yellow brick building; his father worked in the Navy Pay Office here, and the area is featured in a number of his novels including Pickwick Papers and David Copperfield. Chatham boasts several 18th century houses and its Town Hall at the foot of Dock Road has a beautiful scale model of the Victory and mayor's chain which contains material worn by the Doges of Venice and said to be over a thousand years old. Also on Dock Road is the Medway Heritage Centre, occupying the disused St Mary's Church; the exhibits in the nave and aisles of the former church relate the story of the Medway from prehistoric to modern times. To the east of the Centre, across Dock Road, is Fort Amherst and the Great Lines, the complex system of fortifications that underline the town's strategic importance, and from the war memorial at the summit there is a tremendous view of the Medway and its surroundings. Three other of the town's institutions should be mentioned. The former HMS Pembroke, a Navy training base at Chatham for officers and ratings, later became part of the University of Greenwich and is to be found off Central Avenue a little to the east of Dock Road; the town is the home of the Royal School of Military Engineering, housed in Brompton Barracks on the hill above the dockyard; and not far from Brompton Barracks is the Royal Engineers Museum in Prince Arthur Road, relating the story of military engineering from Caesar's time. In latter years the town has enjoyed thriving electronics and cement industries. There are towns called Chatham in the USA and Canada, and the New Zealand-owned Chatham Islands, named after the 1st Earl of Chatham, Pitt the Elder, are to be found in the south-west Pacific. Chatham-and-Dover is late 19th century rhyming slang for "give over," while the London-Chatham-Dover railway line, which you may well utilise to access the Kent coast if you are doing the walk in day trips, was somewhat unflatteringly nicknamed the London Smashem and Turnover!!

***Rochester** is the only cathedral city on your Kent coastal pilgrimage, and a place of immense historical interest. In fact although it boasts a cathedral it is no longer officially a city, having been demoted from city status in May 2002 owing to an administrative oversight! Its name is derived from "Hrofe-Caestre" meaning "camp of Hrof or Roffa,"Roffa being a pre-Christian Saxon warlord. The Romans had a stronghold here called Durobrivae - traces of the Roman walls survive - and the town was re-fortified by the Saxons in around 600. The cathedral was founded by the Saxon King Ethelbert in 604 and consecrated by St Augustine, although the present building is Norman, having been rebuilt from 1077 by Gundulf, Bishop of Rochester; there is a tower named after Gundulf, built in the 12th century after Gundulf's time, and about 50ft of the tower still stands. The cathedral has a particularly fine library which contains the Textus Roffensis dating back to 1115, Coverdale's 1535 Bible, the 1539 Great Bible and numerous ancient documents, while the Norman west doorway of the cathedral, with its very decorative carving, is unique in England. The west front dates from about 1160 and much of it was restored in the late 19th century, but the doorway below it is undoubtedly the original entrance used when the cathedral was consecrated in 1130. Extension to the fabric was made possible by generous offerings to the shrine of William of Perth, a baker of strong faith who was murdered close to Rochester in 1201 during a pilgrimage and who is buried in the cathedral; miracles are said to have taken place at his tomb and he was canonised in 1256. Other features of particular interest in the cathedral include its crypt with medieval graffiti* *scratched on the piers, the splendid collection of memorials in the south transept, the fine paintings on the choir walls, the 13th century choir stalls which are the earliest in Britain, the intricately carved 14th century chapter room door, and approximately 200 heads carved as ceiling bosses or corbels and depicting characters from the Middle Ages.*

Just opposite the cathedral is the keep of a Norman castle. It was Gundulf who built the castle and the line of the outer walls can be attributed to him, but the keep, a really splendid sight as you emerge from the cathedral's west door, was built by William de Corbeuil, Archbishop of Canterbury, at the end of the 1120's. The castle, built to defend the crossing of the Medway, was besieged twice in the 13th century; barons rebelling against King John held the castle for almost 2 months against the king's siege weapons in 1215, and Simon de Montfort besieged it unsuccessfully in 1264. The keep - all that remains of the original castle - is the largest such construction in England, with a height of 128ft, five storeys, and walls that are 12 ft thick. It is possible to climb up the keep, view the site of the great hall, living quarters and chapel, and obtain a great view of the Medway. Other buildings of interest in Rochester include the Bishop's Palace just south of the cathedral and lived in by Bishop John Fisher who was executed at the order of Henry VIII; the gabled and timbered Old Hall behind the keep on Boley Hill, where Henry VIII is said to have met his future wife Anne of Cleves; the 17th century red-brick Guildhall, housing the town's principal museum; King's School which was founded by Henry VIII in 1541; the 16th century Restoration House over the Maidstone Road; the early 18th century Corn Exchange, given to the town by the wonderfully named admiral Sir Cloudesley Shovell; the Tudor brick-built Eastgate House containing the Charles Dickens Centre (see below); and, in the cathedral Close, seven red-brick Georgian houses known as Minor Canon Row, with the 14th century Prior's Gate just behind. The whole of the High Street is a joy from start to finish, with many fine old buildings and an interesting selection of shops and eateries which make a nice contrast to the bland chain stores and cafes of many other High Streets. That said, Rochester is no staid museum piece: it is a bustling workaday town, with industries that include aeronautical, electrical and mechanical engineering, cement, paper, and paint and varnish.

Like Chatham, Rochester has a very strong association with Charles Dickens. As stated above, he lived in neighbouring Chatham when he was a boy, and Rochester figures in his works, under its own and other names, more often than any other place except London. Other names used by him for the town included the not very flattering Dulborough and Mudfog. In 1856 he bought a house nearby called Gad's Hill Place two miles or so to the north-east of Rochester, which was to be his home for the rest of his life. His final book, the unfinished The Mystery Of Edwin Drood, was largely set in Rochester under the name of Cloisterham, while Rochester was Pip's home in one of his most famous works, Great Expectations. The cathedral has a memorial to the author, and there is a Charles Dickens Centre in Eastgate House. Rochester has in recent years become well known for its Dickens festival, with hundreds of local citizens dressing up in Dickensian costume.

SECTION 12 - **ROCHESTER TO ALLHALLOWS-ON-SEA (OPTIONAL DETOUR TO ISLE OF GRAIN)**

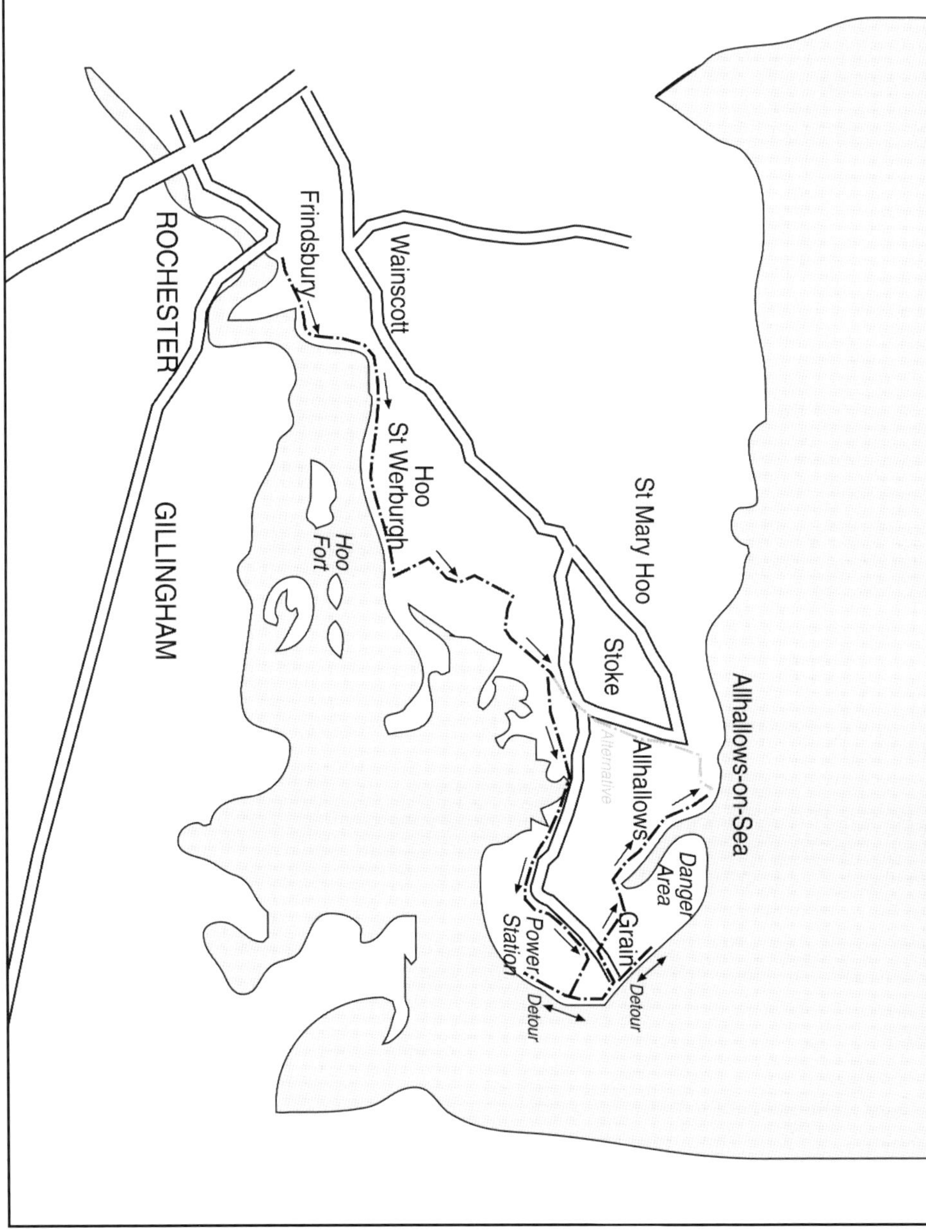

SECTION 12 - **ROCHESTER TO ALLHALLOWS-ON-SEA** (OPTIONAL DETOUR TO ISLE OF GRAIN)

Distance:	12 miles minimum (Up to 6 extra miles for the detour to Grain).
Route:	Rochester - Strood - Upnor - Kingsnorth - Lower Stoke - (Grain detour) - Allhallows-on-Sea.
Map:	OS Explorer Sheet 163.
Public Transport:	Excellent train services linking Rochester with both London Victoria (fastest) and Charing Cross. Regular trains from Strood to Rochester, Gravesend and London Charing Cross via Dartford. Regular buses linking Grain and Allhallows-on-Sea with Rochester and Strood.
Conditions:	This section poses some interesting logistical challenges and you should read the text carefully in order to identify them. Although the actual walking is largely straightforward and enjoyable, notwithstanding some unavoidable tarmac crunching, there are a number of "ifs and buts" and advance planning is essential. If you do your homework carefully, you should find it an immensely rewarding, if sometimes rather surreal, experience.
Refreshments:	See Appendix.

It will be hard to pull yourself away from Rochester's delights, but you may be motivated to do so by the prospect of returning to the open sea towards the end of this section. Continue north-westwards along the High Street to its very end, arriving at a busy road junction, but maintain your north-westerly direction to cross the Medway via the road bridge; the pedestrian walkway is on the extreme left (upstream) side of the bridge. Having walked beside the Medway and its inlets for so many miles, it is nice finally to get a proper look at it from above, and to realise that you are now able to start heading back towards the coastline proper. After you have crossed the bridge, use the subway immediately over the other side to cross the very busy A2. This is as close as you will get to the centre of Strood, a town which has in the past boasted thriving fishing, quarrying and barge-building industries, but which aesthetically is somewhat nondescript. Strood's name means "marshy ground overgrown with brushwood" and it is suggested that the legend that men of Kent were born with long tails, as a punishment for the murder of Thomas a Becket in 1170, had its origins in Strood. Arguably the town's most interesting feature is Temple Manor, owned by English Heritage; noteworthy for the fine vaulting in its undercroft, it was built for the Knights Templar in about 1240 and later became a farmhouse. Emerging from the subway, go very briefly back towards the bridge then turn sharp left into Canal Road, passing under the railway and turning right to reach a very pleasant promenade area beside the Medway. Canal Road is named after the old Thames and Medway Canal, which dates back to the start of the 19th century; it was abandoned in 1845 and subsequently was filled in and used as a railway track. Follow the promenade, admiring the really excellent views across the river and ahead to Frindsbury Church which with its square flint tower and shingled spire is perched proudly on a bluff high above the river. Strood Station, standing on marshland filled with chalk excavated for the canal, is clearly signposted to the left.

Continue beside Canal Road, soon coming to a pub. Pass round the left side of the pub then follow the signposted Saxon Shore Way to thread your way round the backs of houses, shortly arriving at Commissioners Road. Whilst it might seem more logical to turn right into this road, do not do so, for it leads into a large industrial estate built on a large spit of land where the Medway describes an extravagant meander. You must forsake the Medway briefly, crossing the road and following the Saxon Shore Way quite steeply up a footpath on to the cliffs you saw from Canal Road, beside the old Frindsbury quarry. You pass just to the east of Frindsbury Church of which you got such a splendid view on your riverside walk at Strood, and arrive at a junction with Parsonage Lane. Turn right into the lane. You soon pass a footpath going off to the left; immediately beyond this path the road bends right, and as it does so, look out for a signed footpath leading off to the right. Follow this path downhill to a crossing of the A289 which leads on to Medway Tunnel, cross the dual carriageway as indicated with immense care, then bear right along the footpath signed Upnor. The path keeps the main road to the right and a sewage works to the left, but in no time at all you arrive at Upper Upnor where you become reunited with the Medway and things take a definite turn for the better. Go forward to the bottom end of the tiny High Street, with fine views ahead of you to the castle which you will remember seeing from St Mary's Island in the previous section. Turn left into the lovely cobbled High Street which, with its charming weather-boarded houses, is a real delight following the soulless walk from Frindsbury; access to the castle is clearly signposted off the High Street.

Upnor Castle

The river Medway having become an important haven for the Royal Navy by the middle of the 16th century, the castle at Upnor was ordered to be built by Queen Elizabeth I in 1559 to protect the fleet anchored here. The only time that the castle, completed in 1565, was tested was on the occasion of a Dutch invasion of the Medway in 1667, and following the failure of

Standing guard over the Medway, Upnor Castle was built in 1559 but the defences mounted in and round the castle failed to ward off Dutch invasion a century later.

the defences hereabouts to prevent the capture or destruction of several British ships, the castle declined into a powder magazine, general storehouse and museum. Of interest to today's visitor is its good solid outer wall, built of stone much of which was taken from Rochester Castle; its courtyard with a pair of Turkey oaks that are said to have grown from acorns brought back from the Crimean War; its bastion commanding fine views across the Medway; and the castle museum containing a detailed overview and exhibits of Medway defences down the years as well as a collection of Romano-British pottery.

Continue up the High Street to a T-junction with Upchat Road. Turn right into this road and follow the path to the right of the road for what is a rather frustrating walk to Lower Upnor, with the castle grounds and views to the Medway screened from you by high walls. It is a relief to arrive at Lower Upnor where an obvious path takes you along the quayside, past the training ship Arethusa and the Medway Yacht Club, and on to the beach beyond. Here you arrive at your first area of potential logistical difficulty on this section, for the Medway is tidal at this point and an hour either side of high tide the walk from here to Hoo Marina may be impassable. Tide tables should be available from the tourist information centre in Rochester but if you find you have miscalculated it's probably best just to sit it out, rather than taking up time and energy to find and follow an alternative inland route. The beach walk is enjoyable, with woodland to your left and views across the Medway to the right, and providing the weather is kind, you should enjoy good views to St Mary's Island and other landmarks you passed by on the previous section. In due course you arrive at the very large Hoo Marina, a large and straggling assembly of rivercraft and housing; the path through the marina is quite easy to follow, and the Saxon Shore Way signposts will reassure you if you're in doubt. A short way to the north (left), and accessed via Vicarage Lane, is the village of Hoo St Werburgh, a rather sprawling village but boasting a number of shops, a pub and church, and containing the relics of a Georgian village in its centre. It is good to get past the marina, and a really fine walk ensues along a green embankment path, with lovely views to the Medway on your right and across the open countryside to your left, the church spire of Hoo St Werburgh a particularly prominent feature. This whole area, separating the Medway from the Thames (which you will reach not far beyond Grain) is known as the Hoo Peninsula. Just beyond Hoo St Werburgh you say a temporary farewell to the Saxon Shore Way, which cuts across the peninsula, and you will not meet it again until you reach Cliffe, in the next section.

Ahead of you is the vast Kingsnorth Power Station complex dominated by its massive chimney; whatever you may think of late 20th century industrial architecture, it is indisputably a most impressive construction, built on the site of a station where airships were built in the First World War. Follow the embankment right up to the fence marking the boundary of the complex, then, unable to continue alongside the river, turn left to follow along the west side of the fence, heading north-west. Initially you will need to go back on yourself to cross a channel directly ahead of you, and will thereafter have to deviate slightly from the fence to negotiate some of the little pools and streams, but the way becomes easier and firmer as you continue to head inland from the Medway, keeping as close to the fence as possible. The fence-side path now matures into a very pleasant country road which you follow in the same direction, now leaving the fence and the power station complex behind. You need to continue along the country road which bends slightly left, and will

The quiet cobbled main street of Upnor, leading down to the Medway, has a distinctly Mediterranean feel in the height of summer.

soon reach a junction with Eshcol Road going off to the right. Turn right into Eshcol Road and follow it; it has a lovely quiet country feel to it initially, but shortly you pass the Kingsnorth Power Station complex approach road going off to the right. Ignore this and continue along Eshcol Road, then when this road bends sharply left, leave it by a service road that proceeds just east of north, keeping the buildings of Kingsnorth Industrial Estate to your right. This service road soon swings sharply right; almost immediately it has done so, look for and join a signed footpath going off to the left, and proceed gently uphill, crossing a mineral railway that provides a link between the main Gravesend-Strood line at Higham and the Isle of Grain. Looking ahead the scene is serene and pastoral, but glancing back you are staring straight at the stark Kingsnorth Industrial Estate buildings! Follow the path which proceeds pleasantly north-eastwards across a gentle hillside, soon arriving at a road at the hamlet of North Street.

Work, rest and play....the peaceful waters of Stoke Creek and its leisure craft with the stark backdrop of Kingsnorth Power Station which is a prominent feature along much of this section.

Turn right on to the road at North Street and follow it initially south-eastwards, keeping to it as it swings sharply left and proceeds north-eastwards, passing over a stream. Shortly you reach a crossroads with two tracks, the left turn leading to Tudor Farm, but you follow the track that branches off to the right here, down to the railway crossing which is protected by gates which may be locked. They are sturdy enough to climb over - it is suggested you use the hinge end rather than the lock end - and having done so, go forward to arrive at a clear green path*. If you are precluded for whatever reason from climbing the gates, or simply feel uneasy about doing so, you could return to the road, follow it to Creek Lane, the next right turn, and go down the lane and over the railway via the Stoke Creek Crossing. You could then either turn right along the path and follow it to the locked gated crossing and be reunited with the approved route at * above, or turn left to continue towards your ultimate objective. From the

asterisked point, turn left to continue, although you could detour right as far as the gates that mark the eastern border of the Kingsnorth complex and beyond which access is not permitted, returning to the asterisked point the same way.
After this rather fiddly walking, the going is now excellent as you proceed north-eastwards along a clear green path, and there is a huge amount to see and enjoy. To your right is the Medway and a vast number of little spits, inlets, salt marshes pools and creeks; in short, it is a classic estuarine landscape and is very popular with visitors. There are excellent views to the very pretty village of Stoke just the other side of the railway, and there is also a little light aircraft hangar to your left from which you may get free entertainment, particularly at weekends or holiday times, in the form of tiny planes taking off and landing here. Beyond the sheds of the aircraft hanger is a much larger arch-shaped silver corrugated iron building, the headquarters of Medway Microlights, and just beyond that you will reach a junction of paths+, the estuary-side path swinging sharply to the right, and a path going off to the left leading almost immediately to a railway crossing and the village of Lower Stoke just beyond.
It is now decision time. Ahead of you is the Isle of Grain: there will be no difficulty in accessing the village of Grain on foot, and although there is some tough walking including an annoying 2-mile stretch of very dull road marching, the reward is the possibility of a quite fantastic walk beside the Medway Estuary. You will get a grandstand view of the confluence of the Medway and Thames, and watch as both flow out into the open sea. You will also get to see the village of Grain and its surrounds, which are fascinating from an historical and ornithological perspective. But - and it is a big but - it may not be possible to make a pedestrian link between Grain and Allhallows-on-Sea, at the end of this section. This is because much of the only available road or path linking these two places is not a public right of way and access may be denied or impossible; the latter part of the road section is owned by the Ministry of Defence, and a section of track beyond it is protected by gates which may be locked, with future usage of the surrounding land unclear at the time of writing. Effectively, then, you have three choices, and you must make your choice now. Option one is to walk on to Grain, and chance it as far as the walk on to Allhallows-on-Sea is concerned; option two is to walk on to Grain and then backtrack to Lower Stoke; and option three is to miss out Grain altogether (although you could take a bus ride there from Lower Stoke and back again should you wish to visit the village and its remarkable surroundings) and proceed directly to Allhallows-on-Sea. The instructions for the three options are set out individually below.
If you have decided upon options one or two, ignore the path to the left at + going to the level crossing gates, and swing to the right on the "main" path. You will now enjoy a quite delightful walk along this excellent and well-defined footway, keeping the Medway to your right and a succession of long thin pools to your left. You meander pleasantly south-eastwards then swing north-eastwards, getting to within a stone's throw of the main A228 Rochester to Grain road; although you don't actually join the

road here**, you can access it and turn left on to it to return to Lower Stoke should you have had second thoughts about continuing towards Grain (see directions for option three below). Assuming you wish to plough on, keep the road to your left and continue along the path which then describes a giant U, swinging southwards then, as if afraid of straying too far from the road, swinging north-eastwards again to return to the road. It is lovely walking: although the stark industrial complexes of the Isle of Grain are looming up ahead of you, the immediate surroundings are a vast expanse of little pools, channels and creeks, with its attendant excellent bird and plant life. The views are quite tremendous and although the traffic noise on the busy A228 may slightly spoil the sense of isolation, you can feel amazingly alone and there is definitely something of a surreal feel to this part of the walk.

Having returned to the road, you will see that the path comes to an end and you are now forced on to the road for the remaining 2 miles to the edge of the village of Grain; once on the road, and faced almost at once by a succession of formidable industrial complexes, you can consider yourself to be on the Isle of Grain. When the Isle of Grain got its name, first recorded in 1610 and meaning "gravelly or sandy ground," it was literally an island, with some evidence of both Iron Age and Roman occupation, but it has since been cemented to the mainland by a mixture of sand, mud and silt, and it is now impossible to see where it actually starts and finishes. The power station here was, when it opened in the 1950's, the largest oil-fired power station in Europe. The riverside round here is strictly out of bounds, industrial estates abounding, and you must now just keep your head down and get on with the tarmac crunching with nothing of interest to see on either side of the road. You may draw some wry amusement from Pevsner's assertion that "no doubt it was the very remoteness (of the Isle of Grain) that let the refiners think that they had no duty to design and group their buildings decently." The

Though there are prettier pubs on your coast walk, the British Pilot with its distinctive inn sign is a welcome amenity as you arrive at Allhallows-on-Sea.

road swings sharply left, now demoted to a B road, and proceeds north-eastwards, at length leaving the industrial complexes behind and going across countryside to approach the village of Grain.

As you draw near to the village, you will see a road going off to the right, signposted Grain Power Station, and you turn right to follow this road; sadly this is another depressingly dull slog, but at least there is a proper pavement and there will not be the same volume of traffic. The road bends to the right and seems to be coming to a dead end, with the gated power station complex immediately ahead of you, but just before the gate you will see a track going away to the left. It looks unpromising, but follow it; shortly the track swings sharp left (north-eastwards) and then sharp right to reach a T-junction with Port Victoria Road. Turn right on to this road and follow it southwards, reaching a track crossroads in a few hundred yards at which you turn left (eastwards) and follow the track to arrive at the Medway again. If you are pushed for time you could simply turn left on to the estuary-side path heading northwards, but I strongly recommend - especially as you have come this far - that you turn right and follow the estuary-side path southwards and then south-westwards, until forbidding signs and fencing that mark the industrial complex and jetty of Cockleshell Hard stop you in your tracks. You are then forced to backtrack, and follow the estuary-side path back to where you joined it, and on beyond it, heading slightly west of north back towards Grain village. On a clear day, this will be one of the most memorable pieces of your Kent coastal walk. You will get a splendid view upstream to the peninsulas around Rainham, and should also identify the Kings Ferry Bridge over the Swale; there are good views over to the Isle of Sheppey; but more excitingly, looking northwards, you will get your first view of the Thames and will see the confluence of the Medway with that great river, and the mouths of both as they reach the open sea, visible for the first time since Sheerness (or since the mouth of Faversham Creek if you left out Sheppey). As you head northwards again towards Grain village, you will also be able to see Southend-on-Sea on the north side of the Thames Estuary. On a more prosaic note, you may either love or hate the power station which watches over you to your left throughout this piece of walking!

In due course you have the choice between a grassy path, raised slightly from the shore level, and a concrete promenade, both of them arriving at an open space and a small parking area with information board. The board informs you of the rich variety of bird and plant life to be enjoyed here, including oystercatcher, redshank and grey plover among feathered visitors, and sea clover to be found on the shore itself. Despite the grim industrial surroundings, the authorities have clearly worked hard to make this a pleasant place for both locals and visitors to enjoy, with a number of seats as well as the well-defined path and promenade. The continuous route turns left here to pick up Grain High Street (B2001) which you can easily locate, it being just beyond the conspicuous village church that you see to your left. It is, however, possible to continue along a rough estuary-side path for just over a quarter of a mile beyond the open space, initially along a mini clifftop and then down through an area of rough grass, separated from the foreshore by some stone anti-tank defences left from World War 2. For obvious reasons this section of shoreline was of very considerable strategic importance, and a number of military defences were established here in the mid-19th century; the area also has an association with smuggling. Unfortunately, the path comes to an abrupt end as ahead of you is a military range, access to which is strictly barred, and you are forced back to the open space in order to join the B2001, following it south-westwards into Grain village itself.

Shortly you pass the church of St James which is to your left. This is the only building of real historical interest in the village, and its exterior has a certain dignity and impressiveness; it boasts Norman nave walling, aisles that were added shortly before 1200, and an Early English chancel, the interior of which is remarkable for its many recesses. Continue past some nondescript housing estates and playing fields to reach the village centre with its welcome pub, the Hogarth Inn (note the unusual inn sign), and a useful Co-op store. Of even more potential use is the bus stop more or less opposite the Co-op, the hourly buses 7 days a week between here and Gillingham via Strood, Rochester and Chatham providing a lifeline for locals and possibly you too!

It is now decision time again. Should you wish to attempt option one, walk on past the Co-op, bearing right at the T-junction with Chapel Road and then right again into West Lane. All is well to begin with, the road heading initially north then swinging north-west, but as you reach Rose Court Farm you become aware of forbidding signs marking the boundaries of the military ranges to your right, and you will note a road sign indicating that only MOD personnel and residents have right of access. Tantalisingly your ultimate objective for this section, Allhallows-on-Sea, is clearly visible ahead, and there are good views over the little peninsula on which you are now walking, the views stretching to the Thames and its mouth. You reach a barrier and a sentry's cottage - a sign ordering visitors to report to the sentry hardly makes you feel any more welcome - but if you are undeterred (and unchallenged!) walk a few yards beyond the barrier and you will see a green embankment ahead of you and to the left, with a rather unpromising track just before it, also on your left. Leave the road by means of this track, follow it forward to pass through or over a gate which may or may not be locked, and then continue along the track until you meet another track coming from the left, with a row of pylons beyond. Do not be tempted to go left under the pylons, but bear right, aiming for a gate a couple of hundred yards ahead, rounding the south edge of Yantlet Creek as you walk. You either surmount or pass through the gate, almost immediately arriving at a T-junction with a legitimate public footpath; heaving a sigh of relief in the knowledge that it is plain sailing from here on to Allhallows-on-Sea, turn right and follow the path, keeping Yantlet Creek to your right. In due course you arrive at the Thames, signalling that you really are now on the home stretch as far as your Kent coast walk is concerned, and a well-earned pint is barely a mile away. You swing left, now walking beside the Thames, and soon arrive at a junction of paths;

although your route is straight on, there is a path here heading off the embankment to the left and down to a gate, beyond which a track leads you shortly to the British Pilot pub and a bus stop with good bus connections to Grain, Strood and Rochester. Walkers following options two or three will use this path to access the Thames-side path from Lower Stoke and Allhallows. The main route, whichever option has been followed, continues beside the Thames, with fine views across the river to Southend and the south Essex countryside, towards the very obvious Allhallows-on-Sea caravan park.

WARNING - as I hope I have made clear already, there is no guarantee that you will escape challenge and/or an order to backtrack should you attempt the walk from West Lane to the western side of Yantlet Creek. Neither my publishers nor I accept any responsibility for any inconvenience, expense or loss arising from your doing so. YOU ATTEMPT IT AT YOUR OWN RISK. It is not a public right of way and it may be that steps will be taken to render access completely impossible in months or years to come. BE CAREFUL, AND LEAVE IF ORDERED TO DO SO.

If you have decided on option two, or been forced to resort to it by virtue of option one failing, your starting point is back at the Co-op in Grain village, so if you have tried option one and failed, you will have to retrace your steps along West Lane to the Co-op. There are no other possibilities. At the Co-op you must decide whether to walk or bus it back to Lower Stoke; the bus service, from the stop directly opposite the Co-op, is good and regular, even on Sundays, and you will find yourself back in Lower Stoke in the space of a ten-minute ride. The bus stops right in the middle of the village, by the Nags Head pub. If you are a purist, for whom any mechanical aid is an anathema, you will need to follow the High Street past the Co-op, turning right at the T-junction, soon reaching the power station turn-off and then continuing back along the road, effectively retracing your steps. Having left the industrial complex behind you, and parted company from the Isle of Grain, you will then need to decide whether you are going to follow the footpaths you took from Lower Stoke to the edge of the industrial area, or stick to the road. If you decide on the former, simply return to the "decision time" point marked with a + sign above, and follow the instructions below as given to "option three" travellers. If you stick to the road, simply turn right as indicated off the road to arrive at Lower Stoke, quickly reaching the Nags Head in the village centre. Of course, you could do a bit of both, returning to the road for a shorter walk into Lower Stoke when the path returns to it at the point marked ** above, and following the option three directions below.

For those who decide on option three, leaving out Grain altogether, turn inland at + and cross the level crossing; the crossing is protected by gates which may be locked, although there are signs beside the gates implying that access is permitted. Having gone through, or over, the gates and across the railway, go forward along the path, almost immediately arriving at a T-junction with Burrows Lane. Turn right and follow the lane, soon reaching another road junction with a road going off to the right that leads to the main road; take that right turn and go forward to the main road, cross it with care, then turn right and shortly left up Lower Stoke High Street. You pass a couple of shops, arrive at a T-junction with Grain Road, the Nags Head pub to your right, and turn left into Grain Road. (NOTE: If the level crossing gates at the start of this option are locked and you are unable or unwilling to cross them, you will need to follow options one and two as far as the point marked ** above, turn left on to the road and follow it back to Lower Stoke, bearing first right into Grain Road and soon arriving at the Nags Head.)

Both option two and option three travellers now need to follow Grain Road away from the Nags Head in a north-westerly direction, soon reaching a road junction with a church on the corner; turn right here on to Allhallows Road, and simply follow this road out of Lower Stoke, going forward into Stoke Road and heading just east of north. In just under a mile from Lower Stoke you reach the village of Allhallows, dominated by its church of All Saints. The church, in an attractive semi-rural setting, has some fine Norman features, a 14th century chancel screen, and a south doorway that is described by Pevsner as "abnormally richly moulded." Just beyond the church, which lies immediately to the right of your road, you reach a T-junction with Avery Way; turn right and follow Avery Way, passing the village school and a parade of shops including what may be a most welcome takeaway! You are now approaching Allhallows' sister, Allhallows-on-Sea, a straggling village dominated by its massive caravan site and at one time a hugely popular resort. Take the next turning on the right, effectively an extension of Avery Way, and proceed downhill past lines of modern housing; there is one striking red-brick building on the right which stands out from the rest and looks as though it might once have been a hotel. Shortly you see to your left the welcome British Pilot inn, where the road ends, but you continue along a signed track, proceeding in the same (easterly) direction, and reaching a gate which you pass through and go forward to arrive at the Thames-side path. At long last you are reunited with the option one route. If you've followed options two or three it is possible for you to turn right and follow the Thames downstream for a short way before the path swings to the right to set off along the banks of Yantlet Creek; if you have decided to miss the Isle of Grain it really is worth making this detour, with views to the mouth of the Thames which, weather permitting, will not be surpassed elsewhere on your journey. Then backtrack and start your Thames-side walk towards the caravan park, as indicated in the option one description above.

Whichever option you have followed, continue beside the Thames, watching for a lake to your left which is a very popular spot for holidaymakers and locals; shortly beyond the lake you pass a stone post to enter a more open green area with seating provided and caravans now immediately to your left. This rather complicated section ends here, and should you wish to leave the coast path here, there is easy footpath access back to the shops and bus stop at Allhallows-on-Sea as follows. Immediately upon entering this open green area, turn left down a small embankment to pass just to the left of caravan 31 along a narrow path, going forward to join a metalled pathway that passes to the left of caravan 28 and goes uphill to a crossing road. Turn right and then almost immediately left, past a phone box, along a driveway going uphill to a T-junction; turn left here on to the main road through the caravan site, keeping to the right side of the road and passing a small kiosk, going forward to arrive at Avery Way. The bus stop is just over the road to the right, and the British Pilot pub (where there is another bus stop and bus turning point) is just down the road to the left.

Two reasons why it will be hard to drag yourself away from Rochester: its magnificent Norman cathedral, and its variety of shops and cafes to suit all tastes.

SECTION 13 - **ALLHALLOWS-ON-SEA TO GRAVESEND**

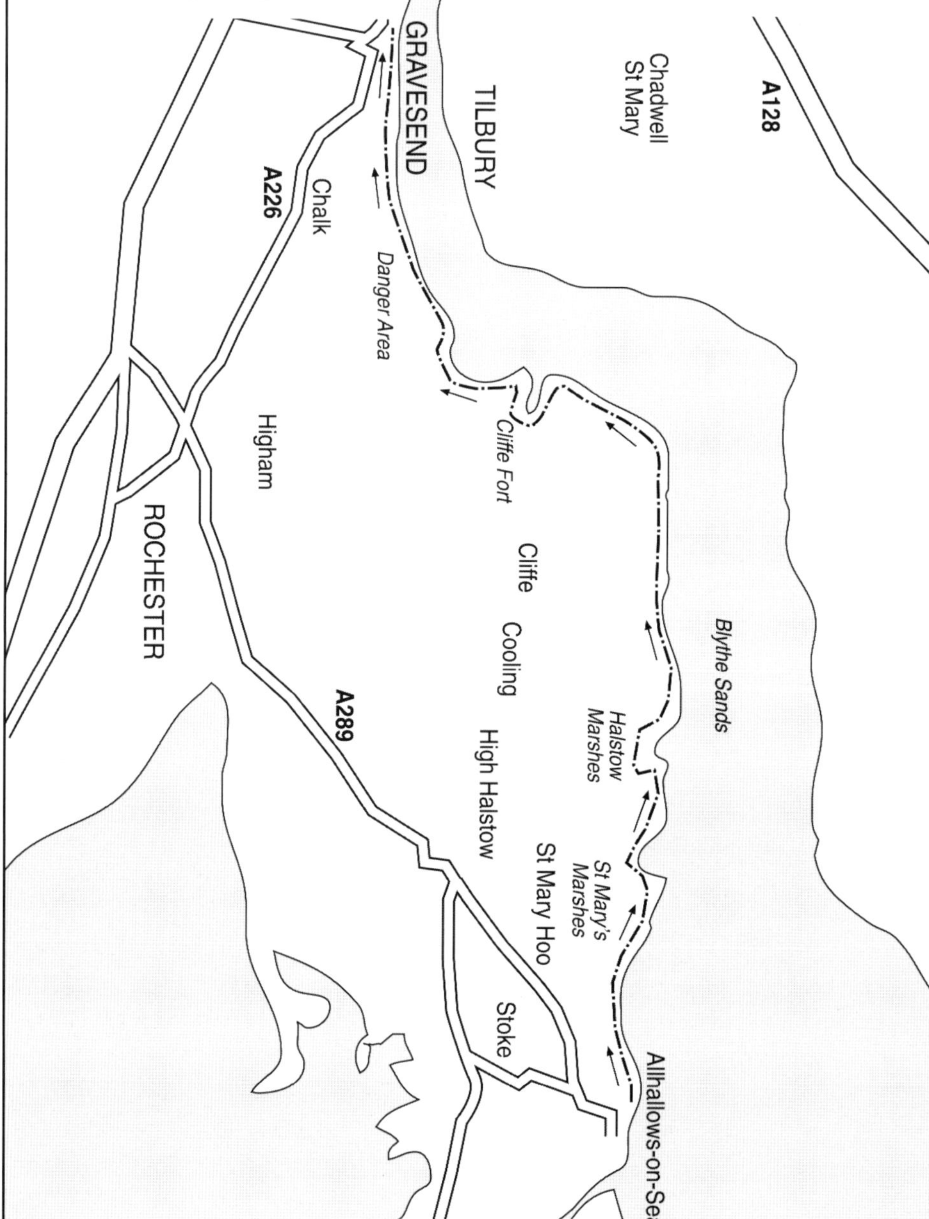

SECTION 13 - **ALLHALLOWS-ON-SEA TO GRAVESEND**

Distance:	16 miles (detour to Cliffe will add 3.5 more miles).
Route:	Allhallows-on-Sea - St Mary's Bay - Egypt Bay - Lower Hope Point - Cliffe Creek - Higham Creek - Shornmead Fort - Gravesend.
Map:	OS Explorer Sheet 163.
Public Transport:	Regular bus service to Allhallows-on-Sea from Rochester and Strood. Limited bus service from Cliffe to Strood and Rochester. Excellent train service from Gravesend to London Charing Cross via Dartford, and to Strood, Rochester and Chatham.
Conditions:	Save a potential difficulty at the very start, this is extremely easy, straightforward and safe walking, virtually all on good footpaths, including long stretches of sea wall. However it is surprisingly remote, and unless you are prepared to make a significant detour to Cliffe some two thirds of the way to Gravesend, there are no amenities, nor any possibilities whatsoever of access to wheeled transport. Be sure, before you start, that you are properly physically equipped to stay the course.
Refreshments:	See Appendix.

The section starts easily enough, with a walk on along the waterfront through the Allhallows-on-Sea caravan park. Enjoying excellent views back to the mouth of the Thames, and across the estuary, you carry on across a greensward, keeping obviously to the river side of it, then follow a narrow concrete path between a fence and a yard to your left, and the wall to your right. Beyond the yard, the obvious path swings left, away from the waterfront, bordered by fencing; when the fencing ends, instead of continuing inland along this path, leave the path by bearing right to walk beside the water. You now need to head for the peninsula directly ahead of you and formed of St Mary's Marshes, where you will be able to pick up an obvious embankment path, but getting to that peninsula presents a potential difficulty. At low tide there will be no problem, in that you can enjoy a walk along the beach and follow it round to the peninsular. However, at high tide sections of beach up to the low bank may be submerged and you will then need to scramble along the bank. This should not pose a difficulty if you are careful, as the bank is reasonably firm and there is a crude path along it in places, but you need to look for cracks, dips and mini-ditches, all of which have some potential for twisting ankles! Marked on some maps is an embankment path which leads away from the shore beside what looks like a small concrete blockhouse built on the beach, then swings westwards, but contrary to indications on the map, it peters out and simply returns you to the shore again. It is also badly overgrown and probably more trouble than it is worth. If the tide is too high to follow the beach, and you are not prepared to scramble over the rough grass on the low bank, the best advice is to wait for the tide to recede. Your wait in any case should not be a long one. Tide tables should be available from local tourist information centres and are also posted on the Internet. Once you have reached the peninsula, the embankment path can be picked up very easily by means of a short sharp climb up the bank just before the end of the beach.

Once you are on the embankment path, things are very easy and will remain so for most of the way to Gravesend. The next few miles are really enjoyable as you proceed confidently along the top of the sea wall on a good path providing grandstand views to the Thames, with its constant stream of shipping including some really impressively large container vessels. You may notice signs on stiles or gates suggesting you are on a "curlews, convicts and contraband" trail! The path goes forward to West Point then swings southwards to negotiate St Mary's Bay, swinging north-westwards and continuing westwards for just under a mile to arrive at Egypt Bay, once notorious for prison hulks that were anchored here. Egypt Bay is a rather more awkward proposition for the walker: the path swings south-eastwards to follow the bay, but don't be fooled

The wide embankment path provides easy walking for much of the first half of the walk between Allhallows-on-Sea and Cliffe, with Old Father Thames for company.

into swinging south-westwards with the embankment, as you will find the way ahead blocked by fencing. You need instead to drop down off the embankment, continuing south-eastwards, aiming for the yellow-topped wooden post and stile ahead; carry on in the same direction then, ignoring a footpath fork going off to the left and remaining on the path, veer first south-westwards then north-westwards, proceeding along a crude embankment. At times it is necessary to leave this embankment briefly in order to pass round large bushes and shrubs, and in due course you need to bear right off the embankment to get through a gate, beyond which the gate the embankment is overgrown and you are forced to follow to the right of it. Shortly you reach the south-west tip of Egypt Bay and are reunited with the main Thames-side embankment again.
The next four miles to Cliffe Creek contain no route-finding difficulties, as the path stays with the sea wall all the way. During these four miles, the river bends south-westwards (or, more accurately, north-eastwards, this being its last significant meander downstream before reaching the sea) and there are views across to the massive industrial complexes of Canvey Island. Meanwhile, to your left there are excellent views across the Hoo Peninsula and most conspicuously the wooded Northward Hill just above High Halstow, and you will also see the houses and very prominent church tower of Cliffe. However, there are problems with remaining on the sea wall because for much of these four miles it is occupied literally by a stone wall with little or no room to walk immediately beside it. Occasionally there are breaks, and in places the overgrown areas beside the stone wall have been cut back, but where this is impossible, it is necessary to use the clearly defined path below and to the left (unfortunately landward) side of the sea wall which sadly offers no views of the river at all, and the rather depressing immediate prospect to your left of ruined or derelict buildings across the fields. If you want to monitor your progress and your swing south-westwards you will need to shin up the green bank from time to time! The solitude is extraordinary and almost macabre when contrasted with the views out to the Thames with its stream of shipping and the industry on the opposite bank. Two other landmarks to look out for are a somewhat incongruous-looking stone memorial by the wall at Lower Hope Point, and a little further down, a pier extending well out into the river.
Shortly beyond the pier, the path below the sea wall (the top of the embankment being absolutely impossible to follow at this point) swings left to proceed eastwards and then south-eastwards along the north side of Cliffe Creek; soon the waters of the very important Cliffe Pool nature reserve appear to the left, and you reach a path going away to the left, with a multi-arrowed signpost at the path junction*. Although the signpost doesn't make this clear, you are here reunited with the Saxon Shore Way which you last saw at Hoo St Werburgh many miles back, and you now have a decision to make. The way on to Gravesend is straight ahead, south-eastwards, at this asterisked junction, but you may wish to bear left to the village of Cliffe, either to end your day's walking and perhaps pick up a bus back to Rochester, or simply to enjoy a pub lunch and a visit to what is a very pretty and historic village with an important nature

reserve. The detour will add an extra three and a half miles to your itinerary. If you still decide to undertake it, follow the path going left from the asterisked junction, along a narrow strip of land between the large expanses of water known as Cliffe Pools, a nature reserve of considerable importance. The bird life here is exceptional: look out for the teal, wigeon, pochard, dunlin, lapwing, shelduck, redshank, turtle dove, nightingale, little egret, avocet, grebe, curlew, hobby, great-crested grebe, little stint, black-tailed godwit, sandpiper and hen harrier. It is hardly surprising that the RSPB were among the most vocal of those opposing the suggestion just a few years ago that a new airport be built in the marshes around Cliffe. There is an abundance of butterflies, the area is also notable for sightings of the water vole and the nationally scarce shrill carder bee, and in the spring there is a profusion of cow parsley and white hawthorn blossom. You arrive at another junction of paths and turn left; follow this path, keeping the water to the left, and shortly after passing through a black-painted gateway you reach a T-junction with an unmetalled lane. Turn right here and follow the lane, picturesquely named Pickles Way, for about half a mile into the village.

Cliffe

History records a settlement at Cliffe as far back as 43 AD, and by the Middle Ages it had become an important port with a population that in the 14th century had reached 3000. The village suffered a great fire in 1520 but in time recovered and its population today is about 6000; local industries have been extremely diverse down the centuries and historically have included not only agriculture - monks grew barley and grazed sheep on the marsh until the late 14th century - but also chalk quarrying and cement working. It boasts a pretty main street with some fine old weatherboarded houses that are very typical of Kent, but its chief glory is its magnificent church of St Helen which dates back to 1260. Its exterior is made up of distinctive alternating bands of flint and ragstone; entered by a very splendid ancient south porch, the church also has a fine interior with an imposing 17th century wooden pulpit, medieval wall paintings, 14th century canopied stone priests' seats, and medieval choir stalls with misericords which would seem more at home in a cathedral or city church. Near the church there is a friendly pub, the Six Bells, serving reasonably priced bar food, and the only refreshment opportunity between Allhallows-on-Sea and Gravesend. Two miles east of Cliffe is Cooling, with a 14th century castle once owned by Sir John Oldcastle on whom Shakespeare based his character Falstaff, and a churchyard which provided the setting for one of the most dramatic scenes in Dickens' Great Expectations, the meeting of Pip and the convict Magwitch. You may however feel that is too much of detour from the coast.

To return to the coast path, simply retrace your steps to the asterisked junction and turn left to rejoin the main route. The main route, which now follows the Saxon Shore Way all the way to Gravesend, continues briefly south-eastwards along the path alongside Cliffe Creek but very shortly leaves this path by means of a much narrower path forking to the right up the little embankment. You could very easily miss this fork, but having climbed the mini-embankment you will see the Saxon Shore Way signpost

Frustratingly the sturdy stone sea wall prevents much embankment walking between Egypt Bay and Cliffe, but it is worth the occasional foray to the wall to view the merchant shipping on the Thames Estuary.

pointing you across the creek and then along a footpath that swings right, westwards, along the south side of the creek. Simply follow this path back to the Thames. Swing left to resume your walk beside the estuary, passing some industrial workings and going forward to the rather ugly grey stone Cliffe Fort, a defensive fort that was built in 1860. Immediately beyond Cliffe Fort you will see a large lake to your left, and the coast path proceeds south-eastwards along a narrow strip of land between this lake on the left and the broad inlet of Higham Creek to your right. After half a mile a path forks off to the left but you keep to the path nearest the creek to your right and then swing south-westwards away from the lake, now heading in determined fashion for Gravesend. Initially you can choose between a low embankment path which is nearer the Thames, or a higher embankment to the left which while not hugging the estuary bank affords better views to the south across Higham Marshes and towards the open country beyond. In due course, at Higham Saltings, the lower path gives out and you are forced on to the higher embankment but near Shornmead Fort, built in the late 19th century by General Gordon, you are directed half right, off the higher embankment; keeping Eastcourt Marshes to the left, you now proceed along the right-hand side of a long greensward protected by fencing on its south side. The greensward can be very muddy in wet weather. Then, with the houses and factories of Gravesend now looming ahead, you rise on to a green embankment once more, heading now resolutely for the town and the end of this long section.

The embankment path proceeds pleasantly on just west of south, initially keeping fields to the left, but before long the surroundings become much more industrial, with

The beautiful church of St Helen, Cliffe, with its superb choir stalls and priests' seats, is certainly worth the detour from the coast path.

jetties and wharves beside you and views over the Thames to Tilbury Power Station. The embankment path ends and you must proceed by mounting steps to a metalled path which you follow past the Ship and Lobster, your first on-route pub since the British Pilot at Allhallows-on-Sea. Shortly beyond the pub, you will observe a road down to your left; the metalled track ahead, although looking promising, does in fact go forward to a dead end, so you will need to bear left to the road, and keeping the Euromix complex to the left, follow the road round to the left, away from the river. Take the next road turning to the right, Wharf Road, following the cycle route sign, then at the west end of Wharf Road, go forward on to a footpath which kinks to the right before widening and becoming a cobbled lane. At the end of this lane you cross the canal and immediately bear right to enjoy a walk along the Gordon Promenade, named after General Gordon of Khartoum who commanded the fort at Gravesend for a time in the late 19th century. Unfortunately at the west end of the promenade you are forced away from the waterfront on to Commercial Road, then having paused for a second to admire the splendidly carved fingerpost telling you the distance to Inverness, you continue briefly along this road to reach a T-junction with The Terrace. Turn right and walk uphill, then take the second right turn into Royal Pier Road which heads north back towards the river; now follow this road as it swings westwards, passing the pretty Royal Terrace Pier which was built in 1842-43, the elegant Clarendon Hotel, the ruins of a 16th century blockhouse, and an old chapel which is now an arts centre. You are now back beside the Thames again. Keeping the river to your right, continue along a path to arrive at a square with the Three Daws pub, a 600-year-old inn with smuggling associations, to your left and the Riva Club to your right. This point marks the end of this section and is as near as you will get to the centre of Gravesend; you can reach the town's many shops and other amenities by turning left past the Three Daws, and going forward to and across the main road.

Gravesend

Gravesend, referred to as Gravesham in the Domesday Book of 1086, developed as a town in the Middle Ages, after local people built a river wall to provide sheep pasture. The wall served to convert the Thames to a navigable waterway which in turn enabled it to thrive as a port, and it did in fact become a port of huge importance, being a centre of trade with the Low Countries and France, the departure point for the Merchant Adventurers and sea voyagers including Frobisher, Cabot and Drake, and the launching point for expeditions by the East India Company, and liners bound for outposts of the British Empire. The town also acquired the sole rights to run the ferry up the Thames known as the Long Ferry or Long Passage; the ferry evolved its own special transport, the tilt-boat, named after the "tilt" or awning which provided shelter for passengers. Early exports included corn, cattle, glassware and also slaves, while today the wharves both here at Gravesend and at neighbouring Northfleet see the unloading of coal, paper and aggregates. It still remains a port of considerable importance, being linked by ferry to Tilbury on the opposite bank of the Thames, and a customs and pilot station for the Port of London; it is here that river pilots take control of ships using the Port of London. The old town was destroyed by fire in 1727, and it was only a century later that the town significantly redeveloped commercially and industrially, but it now boasts extensive industry including engineering, printing, and manufacturing of electrical goods and a range of paper goods, as well as a fine shopping centre. At one time the town was famous not only as a port and for its industry but for its market gardens, especially the local asparagus which was known as "Gravesend grass." Buildings of note in the town include St George's Church, rebuilt in 1731-33 after the fire, with its distinctive pinnacle-topped tower and with a north aisle described by Pevsner as "hideous;" the Town Hall in the High Street, with its fine Doric columns dating back to 1836; the brown-brick Regency Customs House at the east end of The Terrace, built in 1815-16; Milton Chantry in the corner of Fort Gardens, north-east of the Customs House, which although it has an 18th century exterior dates back to the 14th century and became a museum in 1975; and the Gothic clock tower in the town centre, with its gabled clock faces, dating back to 1887.

The town is linked with a number of famous figures. General Gordon of Khartoum, as Royal Engineer Officer in Command between 1865 to 1871, commanded the fort here, the poet Thom Gunn was born in the town, the framing narrative of Joseph Conrad's 1902 novel Heart Of Darkness was set on a ship anchored off the town, and the Native American woman Pocahontas, eponymous heroine of a very popular Disney film released in 1995, died off Gravesend in 1617 when about to return to America. Following her death she was buried in what was the previous church of St George in the town and there is a fine memorial statue of her just outside the church. The Disney film provided a welcome boost to tourism when the film was first released. The first V1 flying bomb to strike Great Britain in World War 2 landed at Gravesend on 13th June 1944.

SECTION 14 - **GRAVESEND TO DARTFORD**

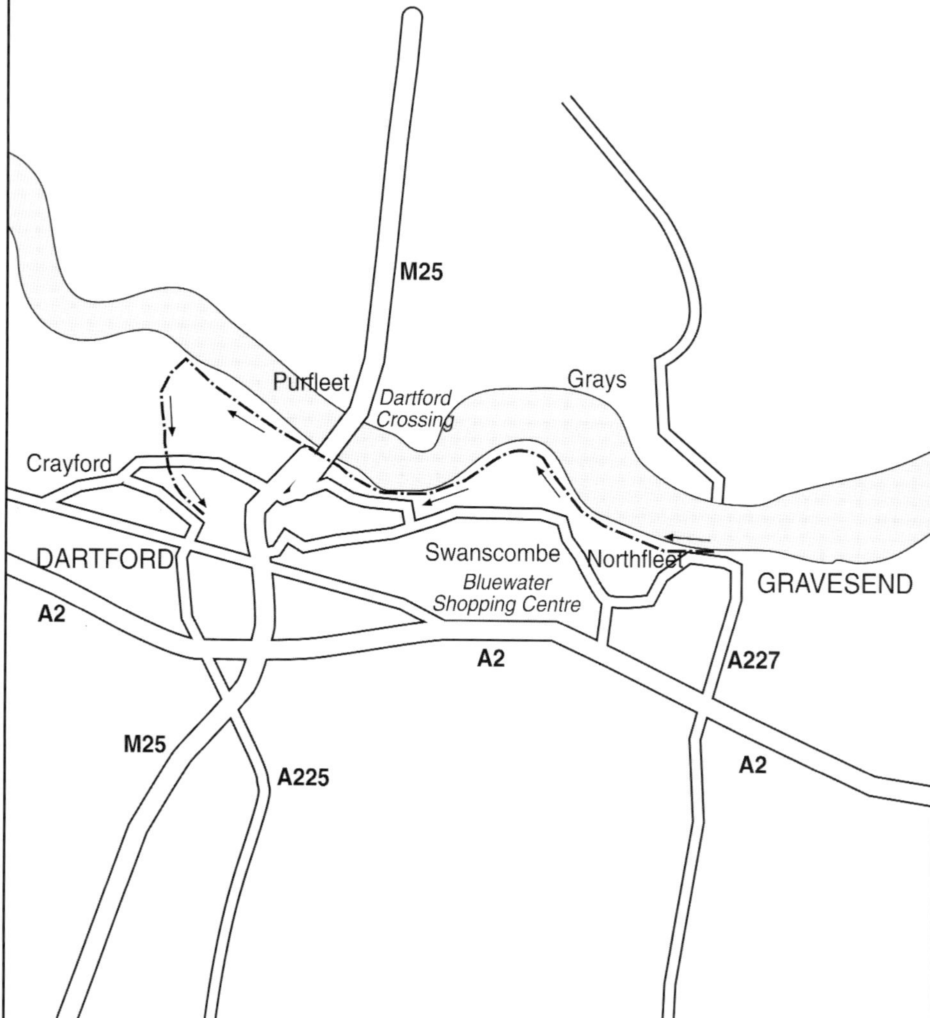

SECTION 14 - **GRAVESEND TO DARTFORD**

Distance:	10 miles.
Route:	Gravesend - Rosherville - Northfleet - Broadness - Greenhithe - Queen Elizabeth II bridge crossing - Darent Valley Path - Dartford.
Map:	OS Explorer Sheet 162.
Public Transport:	Excellent, very regular rail services linking Gravesend, Northfleet, Greenhithe and Dartford, with many trains from all these places to London and Rochester.
Conditions:	This is a walk of two halves, with fiddly and sometimes uninspiring walking as far as Broadness, then splendid riverside walking virtually all the way to the mouth of the Darent which effectively marks the end of the Kent coastline. The walk alongside the Darent to return to civilisation at Dartford is not unpleasant but may feel something of an anticlimax!
Refreshments:	See Appendix.

With loins girded for the final section, leave the little square fronted by the Three Daws pub and the Riva nightclub, and continue along the waterfront by means of a board walk entered at the western end of the square. The board walk, which passes to the right of blocks of modern flats and which can be slippery in wet weather, peters out and it is necessary to backtrack a little to a flight of steps that provides access to a road that in turn leads to the main road, named West Street. Turn right into West Street and go straight on under the bridge, then turn immediately right at the roundabout on the other side into Clifton Marine Parade; follow this road initially, then bear right to take advantage of a new waterfront walk which you can access by bearing right around the side of a new housing development named Baltic Wharf. When the waterfront path ends, bear left to join the waterside road that services the industrial units, passing a rather splendid building, the White House, which is situated to the right and looks somehow out of place in these surroundings! You soon reach a T-junction, turning right here into the road named The Shore. This area is known as Rosherville, named after the entrepreneur Jeremiah Rosher, whose aim it was to create a riverside resort on the site of the chalk quarries that had once existed here; to this end in the 1830's he

Immortalised by Disney but suffering what was far from a fairytale ending in real life, Pocahontas is remembered in Gravesend, the town off which she died in 1617.

built an estate of new houses and a pleasure garden with a zoo, amusements and theatrical entertainments. It was particularly popular with working-class Londoners who used to arrive by boat, and an information board marks the site of the pier used by the day trippers. The area had more practical use during World War 2, when it housed an observation shelter for German parachute mines.

Keep walking along Shore Road; in due course it bends sharply to the left, but you are able to continue beside the water for a little while along the signed cycle route, before being forced away from the water's edge along a narrow path that leads you to Crete Hall Road. Turn right on to this road and follow it, now separated from the river by industrial development, to a mini-roundabout which you cross straight over, keeping to the road. Shortly beyond the roundabout, the road bends sharply right, and a little beyond this right bend, watch carefully for a metalled path going hard left, creating almost a hairpin bend with the road. Take this path which climbs quite steeply to arrive at a T-junction with Northfleet High Street. Northfleet, meaning simply "northern place by the stream"(the stream being a creek of the Thames) is noteworthy for the conspicuous brick tower of its Roman Catholic church, built by Sir Giles Gilbert Scott in 1914, and, in the parish church, the 14th century carved oak screen which is believed to be the oldest in the county. The riverside cement industry developed here, using chalk and clay dug from local riverside pits, and indeed it is impossible to follow the river bank through Northfleet because of the extensive industrial working immediately adjacent to the river at this point. On reaching the High Street, turn right to follow it, continuing past Hive Lane and the rather sad-looking parade of shops called the

Hive, then turn right into College Road and follow it downhill. There is a good view of the Thames as you descend.

At the bottom you reach a T-junction; according to local signposts and the map, you should be able to locate the Cement Industry Heritage Centre just to the right of the T-junction, but at the time of writing the centre appeared not to be open. Your route in fact turns left here into Grove Road which you follow round to the roundabout, passing further industrial workings as you walk. At the roundabout turn right, then take the first turning on the right into Lower Road that goes forward to turn itself into Manor Way, which you simply now follow through another big industrial estate. Fortunately there is a relief now from tarmac crunching as a green embankment path becomes available shortly, proceeding parallel with Manor Way, the path keeping to the left of the road; look out for the massive tall factory chimney to your right as the road, having swung right and left, then swings more gently right and straightens out. Beyond the chimney you appear to be heading straight for another big industrial complex but just beyond the chimney and before you reach the gates, your parallel path, which you continue to follow, drops down to the left of the little embankment and then veers away to the left, round the south side of the complex.

Shortly the path, having struck out across a grassy no-man's land, reaches a T-junction with a wider track, and you now turn right on to this track and follow it. Rising slightly, it reaches a complex track junction at which you find that you are close by the

The sun tries to break through on a winter's morning in Gravesend, looking across to Tilbury Docks. A ferry still links Tilbury and Gravesend today.

waterside again, with excellent views forward to the twin settlements of Swanscombe and Greenhithe, and the prospect of a clear waterside path from here to Greenhithe. You are in fact on the west side of a little salt marsh peninsula called Broadness, a marvellous grassy open space with an extensive network of paths which are not marked on even the larger scale maps. From the track junction mentioned above, you could bear right and follow tracks that would enable you to get up to the top of the peninsula and along a section of its east side; this will afford you a grandstand view of one of the more significant meanders of the Thames as it proceeds seawards, and it is a shame that the factory complex prevents a continuous walk around it. How long you linger in this delightful area, very popular with walkers and bikers, will depend on how much time you've got. If you are in a hurry, you could simply continue forward from the track junction along the waterside path to Greenhithe, but if you have time to enjoy Broadness you may make your way to the top end of the factory complex and hug the bank of the Thames all round the peninsula, only then reuniting yourself with the quicker route and proceeding purposefully towards Greenhithe along what is an excellent riverside path. As you approach Greenhithe, don't be put off by forbidding gates in front of you (at the time of writing these gates marked the entrance to an extensive housing development), but slip down to the right to join a concrete promenade that soon turns into an impressive walkway through a grassy area in front of a major and elegant completed housing development. Then pick your way past further areas of new housing, keeping to the waterfront throughout along specially created paths, before you are forced back on to the picturesque Greenhithe High Street

The highlight of the final section of the Kent coast walk, this is the magnificent Queen Elizabeth II bridge carrying clockwise traffic on the M25 over the Thames since it opened in 1991.

via Frobisher Way. Even then you are able to turn right almost immediately into Sara Crescent to enjoy another waterfront walk, before the crescent returns you to the High Street. Greenhithe is a most attractive place, and it is hard to think that only a short distance away from here is the massive Bluewater shopping complex, one of the largest shopping centres in the country.

Follow the road away from Greenhithe, the road turning inland to arrive at a busy roundabout junction with the A206 Crossways Boulevard; turn right here, passing beside a huge Asda, then beyond the Asda buildings and slip road, and just before the Antalis complex, turn right along a footpath marked Crossways. This passes to the right of the Antalis complex and takes you back to the waterfront. Now the walking becomes easy and straightforward and will remain thus all the way to the end of your journey, with an excellent waterside path available from here to the mouth of the Darent. For much of the way you have a choice between two paths, separated by a little dip; I would recommend that you stick to the one closest to the river, to get the best possible view of the splendid variety of ships and other rivercraft on the Thames. In due course you reach the undoubted highlight of this section, the magnificent Queen Elizabeth II bridge crossing of the Thames, opened in 1991 to ease the congestion in the M25 Dartford Tunnel. You pass directly underneath this tremendous structure, which is the nearest non-ferry crossing of the Thames to the sea, and at the time of opening was the longest cable-stayed bridge in Europe. The going remains straightforward and fast as you proceed away from the bridge, with the river immediately to your right and large industrial works to your left. Beyond the works the countryside opens up a little to the left, with the buildings of Dartford across the fields, while straight ahead the sight of the large sprawling district of Erith, which lies outside Kent, tells you that you are nearly at journey's end. It is good to be in more open country with better and more extensive views than at any time since your walk from Broadness to Greenhithe.

Two miles or so from the Queen Elizabeth II bridge, the way forward beside the Thames is blocked by the river Darent coming from the left; the border between Kent and the borough of Bexley runs along the river at this point and, from its mouth, directly across the Thames, and this therefore marks the end of your walk along the coastline of Kent. Celebration is, however, premature, as you still need to get back to civilisation from here, and this is conveniently effected by means of the well marked Darent Valley Path. Use the obvious path to swing left along the bank of the Darent, following the embankment, and keep going along the embankment path, observing the Darent Valley Path signposts. The path doesn't adhere strictly to the river, but nor does it follow a straight line and meanders quite elaborately (and, if you are footsore from your travels, frustratingly!) before finally climbing to reach the very busy Dartford bypass. Cross this dual carriageway with immense care, using the obvious crossing points, regain the river bank on the other side, and join a straighter more direct riverside path which proceeds pleasantly through meadows initially then into

Dartford. You pass through a gate to enter a concrete area with industrial units, and soon arrive at a footbridge over the Darent; cross the bridge, going forward beyond it along a path to reach a T-junction with Hythe Road, then turn left along Hythe Road to arrive at a busy roundabout. The approach road to Dartford's railway station, with plenteous trains back to London or eastwards to Gravesend, Rochester and Gillingham, is just across the roundabout, and Dartford's town centre, offering plenty of amenities but nothing of real historical interest, is a little way beyond the station approach road.

Now your Kent coastal walk truly is at an end. Whether or not you walked it end to end, or in bits at a time, you will have enjoyed a truly remarkable variety of coastal landscapes, from cheerful resorts to goldmines of history, from serious birdwatching country to massive defensive fortifications, from rocky beaches to towering cliffs, from windswept marshlands to hives of industry. You deserve a nicer town than Dartford to celebrate your achievement, and where better than Rochester, just a few stops down the railway line, with its beautiful High Street and plethora of fine restaurants and teaplaces. Wherever you do celebrate, congratulations: you have walked the coastline of Kent!

APPENDIX

Refreshments

P = pub; F = foodstore(s); C = café(s) and/or restaurants
Section 1 - Dungeness (P), Dymchurch (P,F,C)
Section 2 - Hythe (P,F,C), Folkestone (P,F,C), Dover (P,F,C)
Section 3 - St Margarets At Cliffe (P,C), Kingsdown (P), Deal (P,F,C)
Section 4 - Sandwich (P,F,C), Ramsgate (P,F,C)
Section 5 - Broadstairs (P,F,C), Kingsgate (P), Margate (P,F,C)
Section 6 - Birchington (P,F), Reculver (P,F), Herne Bay (P,F,C)
Section 7 - Whitstable (P,F,C), Seasalter (P,F,C), Faversham (P,F,C)
Section 8 - Oare (P), Conyer (P), Sittingbourne (P,F,C)
Section 9 - Harty (P), Leysdown-on-Sea (P,F,C)
Section 10 - Minster (P,F,C), Sheerness (P,F,C), Queenborough (P,F,C)
Section 11 - Upchurch (P), Rainham (P,F,C), Chatham (P,F,C), Rochester (P,F,C)
Section 12 - Strood (P,F,C), Upnor (P), Hoo St Werburgh (P,F), Lower Stoke (P,F), Grain (P,F), Allhallows-on-Sea (P,F)
Section 13 - Cliffe (P), Gravesend (P,F,C)
Section 14 - Northfleet (P,F), Greenhithe (P,F), Dartford (P,F,C).

Accommodation

The following are accommodation addresses recommended by the AA and Enjoy England. Note that some of them are a little way back from the coast but could certainly be considered if you were using the accommodation as a base for tackling the walk. This list is by no means an exhaustive list of available accommodation: further details are obtainable by contacting one of the tourist information offices below.
Dymchurch - Waterside, 15 Hythe Road, tel 01303 872253; Hythe - Swan, 59 High Street, tel 01303 266236; Folkestone - Beachborough Park, Beachborough, Newington, tel 01303 275432; Dover - Castle, 10 Castle Hill Road, tel 01304 201656; Walmer - Hardicot, Kingsdown Road, tel 01304 373867; Deal - Ilex Cottage, Temple Way, Worth, tel 01304 617026; Sandwich - New Inn, 2 Harnet Street, tel 01304 612335; Ramsgate - Glendevon, 8 Truro Road, tel 01843 570909; Broadstairs - Bay Tree, 12 Eastern Esplanade, tel 01843 862502; Margate - Greswolde, 20 Surrey Road, Cliftonville, tel 01843 223956; Whitstable - Pearl Fisher, 103 Cromwell Road, tel 01227 771000; Faversham - Barnsfield, Fostal, Hernhill, tel 01227 750973; Sittingbourne - Sandhurst, Farm Forge, Seed Road, Newnham, tel 01795 886854; Sheerness - Sheppey Guest House, 214 Queenborough Road, Minster, tel 01795 665950; Rochester - King Charles Hotel, Brompton Road, Gillingham - tel 01634 830303.

Useful Telephone Numbers

National Rail Enquiries - 08457 484950; Tourist Information Centres - Folkestone 01303 258594, Dover 01304 205108, Deal 01304 369576, Sandwich 01304 613565(summer only), Margate 0870 2646111, Herne Bay 01227 361911, Whitstable 01227 275482, Faversham 01795 534542, Rochester 01634 843666, Gravesend 01474 337600.
Website: www.kentattractions.co.uk

Two delightful scenes on the north Kent coast. Above: near Faversham. Below: at Seasalter.